# Carpet Burns
*My Life With Inspiral Carpets*

Tom Hingley

First published by Route in 2012
PO Box 167, Pontefract, WF8 4WW
info@route-online.com
www.route-online.com

ISBN : 978-1901927-54-2

Editors:
Kelly Wood and Ian Daley

Design:
GOLDEN
www.wearegolden.co.uk

Cover Photo:
Ian Tilton
www.iantilton.net

Photos:
Thanks to the following for permission to use their images in the
book: Andreas Andrews, Paul Brownridge, Jo Doran, Jonny Gault,
Brendon Levelli, Maz Seaman, Glenn Routledge, Peter J Walsh,
and the Hingley family archive.

Typeset in Bembo by Route

Printed and bound by CPI Group (UK) Ltd, Croydon, CR0 4YY

A catalogue for this book is available from the British Library

## Devil Hopping

## Keep the Circle

*To the memory of Ronald Hingley,*
*who stepped on people's toes,*
*and to my mother, Ruth Hingley.*

Plane Crash

# I
## *Plane Crash*

# 1

## I see a skull on a stick

On the evening of 20ᵗʰ February 1989 I was watching Tony Wilson's Granada TV show, *The Other Side of Midnight*, when Inspiral Carpets came on playing an instrumental version of 'Directing Traffic'. Wilson then announced that the band needed to find a new singer. However, four hours before the programme went out, Inspirals' manager Binsey Smith had called me and asked me if I would like to come along and audition to be in the band.

At the end of the week I drove up to The Mill and met them. The Mill was full of steel furniture which was being painted with a black paint that hung in the air and made me cough incessantly. I leant up against the carpet-lined wall, holding on to the lyrics on a piece of paper while I sang along to a few of the songs. They invited me back to another session the following day. By the end of the second week I had rehearsed with them four times, yet they still hadn't told me that I had been accepted as the new singer of Inspiral Carpets.

A week later, we were recording the single 'Joe' in Square One in Bury. I did my vocal take in the booth, singing over the backing of bass, drums, guitar and keyboards. While I was in the booth, Graham and Clint heard something in my voice they hadn't recognised before. Returning to the studio's control room, Clint said: 'You've got a bloody lisp.' I replied: 'It's too late – I'm in the band now.'

# 2

# Husband don't know what he's done

Working with Inspiral Carpets was a full-time job, but fitting in with the band was the hardest work of all. The rest of the band, and indeed other local bands, were Northern and working-class, whereas I was Southern and middle-class. Clint, Graham and Craig's Oldham accents could be impenetrable at times. Oldham is physically only seven miles from Manchester city centre, but culturally it is a million miles away. It is at once slapstick and philosophical, demonstrated in the archetypal Les Dawson joke about the place:

> *Lady getting on the bus: 'How much is it to Oldham?'*
> *Bus driver: 'The same price it is to touch them.'*

To say that the rest of Inspirals were piss-takers wouldn't even get close. Lord knows what they made of a nervous lisping southerner in their midst.

My family were a typical Oxford Don's family, if such a thing exists, with a big rambling Victorian house where we camped and snuggled under winter blankets all year long. It was an eccentric existence funded and maddened by my father, Ronald. He wrote books during the night, and slept during the day, maintaining a calculated, formidable, sometimes malevolent presence.

A prodigious talent at languages and with a keen algebraic

mind, my father found himself breaking enigma codes during the Second World War. He worked on the Slavonic-language operation; many of Hitler's submarines were crewed by Ukrainians. He was later an advisor to the government and media on Cold War politics.

He became a Don at St Antony's College, Oxford, specialising in Slavonic studies. His research found him translating the whole of Chekhov's output for the Oxford University Press over a thirty-five year period, truly a life's work. In 1962 he met the anti-Soviet novelist and commentator Alexander Solzhenitsyn after disembarking from an official literature convention under the cover of night and making a secret fifty-mile journey across Russia with his friend Max Hayward. He later translated Solzhenitsyn's novel *One Day in the Life of Ivan Denisovich*.

My father operated in a world where intelligence was of superior importance to social skills and the ability to raise small children. Inherent in this underlying attitude was an unspoken belief that the procreation of ourselves was the total responsibility of our mother and us individually, that the male flower had issued its seed, had been picked up on the wind and touched the stamen in the moment of our creation. There ended his parental responsibility, though he did pay for us all to live.

He himself had been subjected to the vagaries of his own father, a Methodist minister who anecdotally possessed even less empathy for his issue than Dad showed us. Dad, a prodigy of a child, felt embarrassed from an early age by his parents, by their silly superstitious religion, which his rationality and rebellion utterly rejected. A rejection of the spiritual is something that my parents had in common and lived by. I remember being ten years old in church with my mother holding and squeezing my hand. Exiting the church she told me, 'God doesn't exist – I only come to services for comfort.'

My parents' rejection of their Christian values keened me into a rebellion of praising the Lord as loud and as often as possible. My first formal introduction to music was as part of the choir in the local Anglican Church in Marcham. Every Sunday we would walk the mile to the service along a tree-lined path, adjoined by fields and cows. It was there that I would learn to sing and harmonise, and mull over the words in the stout Victorian hymns. Acoustic church singing is the best training any singer can have, particularly in a resonating vaunted stone building. We would walk the mile back to Sunday lunch and gardening duties.

My mother, Ruth Wyatt, was born in China in the Shansi Province in 1930. Her father was a famous doctor and Baptist missionary during the Chinese Civil War. So famous was he that a book describing his good works was published called *Harry Wyatt of Shansi*. He died a tragic death. On 5th May 1938 he was travelling to a district called Guoxian to deliver medical supplies for the clinic he ran in Shansi Province. He was travelling with another missionary, a woman called Beulah Glasby, and a Chinese chauffeur called Hu Shih Fu. On the way they were overpowered by Chinese guerrillas who mistook them for a band of Japanese soldiers – the Japanese were advancing into that region of China at the time. Once the insurgents had shot at and stopped the car, Harry reacted by walking towards the rebels to explain that they weren't Japanese, but all three of the party were shot dead. Sticks for crosses and the words 'man' and 'woman' written on pieces of paper marked the sad graves where they were left.

Upon the death of her father, Ruth was immediately dispatched to a boarding school in Sevenoaks, to a culture and country totally alien to her. The mixture of grief and culture shock must have been very hard to bear. Outside term times, she and her brothers were split up into two groups: the two older brothers, Arthur and Ted, lived with their mother; Ruth and George were housed by their Uncle Redge, a man who seemed to resent the arrival of two small children (not of his making) into his life. Added to these setbacks, she was refused permission to study and enter the family's profession and become a doctor. My mother met and married my father in 1953 to repel the attempts of her own relatives who wanted to co-opt her to a spinster's life, looking after an ill Uncle Redge.

Ruth, a complicated and loving mother, replaced the loss of her father and rejection by her family by raising seven children, of which I was the youngest. In her own quiet persuasive way, she encouraged all of us to be good at one thing in particular. It is often said that in large families you bring up one another and this was certainly true of the Hingleys.

From Peter, my eldest brother, I received kindness and a teasing paternal attention that my father wasn't always exuding. He created the annual election at Easter time of 'Rotten Egg', where all family names were written on pieces of paper and then put into a hat. The first one pulled out was designated to be the holder of the 'Rotten Egg' title, the next drawn out being 'First worst person' followed by the 'Second worst person' then 'First best person' and lastly 'Second best person'. The excitement of this ceremony reduced greatly once we were all old enough not to complain about the titles awarded and Peter's glee dissipated. I am sure the contest came from a dark place in Peter's psyche which rued the day his parents continued to add to their brood.

As a child I was shy, clumsy and slow to learn, possibly exploiting my role as the youngest by trying to prolong the childish state for as long as possible. I shared a room with Andrew, the difficult middle child, who was neglected. He bullied me as a small boy. Even now I am a ready flincher, as are many men with four older brothers and a father who shouted a great deal. Andrew was sixteen when he began to teach himself to play guitar to the soundtrack of Jimi Hendrix's *Axis: Bold As Love*. I can still remember the molten ice cream smear of psychedelia that was 'Castles Made of Sand' heard as an eleven-year-old for the very first time.

Andrew and I formed a project called *Tom and And*. Our trick was to compose ad-libbed songs where Andrew would write the music, and I would add a made-up narrative. The song would normally have a set opening line such as 'Let me take you by the hand'.

Vicky, the first girl and perhaps a little spoilt by my mother, shared a room with my other sister Helen, directly above us in the middle of the house. Vicky followed the pop music of the seventies and her bedroom walls were festooned with pictures of Donny Osmond, David Bowie, The Sweet, Marc Bolan and, of course, David Cassidy; all cut out from *Jackie* magazine. *Jackie* was to my sister what the *NME* would be to punks a few years later, with all the added pain of the 'Cathy and Claire' problem page. Aged six, she used to dress me up as a girl to tease me, but, ever the androgynous proto-pop star, I secretly used to love all the attention and naughtiness of it. An early dream of stardom came at the age of seven, in our neighbour Will Rayson's attic, where we were miming tennis racket guitars, as Marc Bolan and T. Rex.

Helen is my nearest sibling. She is strong willed, and we were very close back then, whether making up song lyrics to the television test card together, or playing with a length of garden hose; one of us with an end to our ear and the other singing into it. Whether she knew it or not, she truly was a musical inspiration to me. We wrote a satirical song together in 1973 called 'Chicken Bones and Children's Voices... Yeah'. I can still sing it, note perfect, and do so at least three times a year down the phone to Helen.

I took a lot of inspiration from my brothers. The second eldest brother, Richard, was intellectually very stimulating. We would have long drawn-out discussions; in one I would have to be a communist arguing for my cause, with Richard portraying a fascist. We would tear the other's argument down, then reverse positions. Martin, third in line, was very thin as a child and bore the politically incorrect nickname of 'Oxfam'. He excelled at painting and I have always looked up to him musically. Martin formed a band with Andrew in 1976 called Ash Tray and The Dogends, and as an eleven-year-old I was fascinated by them. They used to rehearse in the barn next door, which was ancient and was said to contain timber and stone from Abingdon Abbey, pulled down in Henry VIII's reformation. Everyone in the band, apart from Andrew, attended Abingdon School, a direct grant school that brothers Peter, Richard and Martin had won paid scholarships to attend. Twenty years later, Abingdon School would be the launch pad for Radiohead.

I had begun my musical career by trying to learn to play the piano, but I wouldn't practice and didn't progress. Violin was my next failure, then trombone. Each instrument taught me something about singing, though: piano – scales; violin – precision playing; trombone – vocal attack, so I suppose it wasn't a total waste of time. When I was nine years old, I sang in a choir in a musical about Noah's Ark called *Captain Noah and His Floating Zoo* by Joseph Horovitz. I fell in love with being on stage and couldn't sleep all night because of the adrenaline: I had found myself through singing. I knew then that I wanted to perform.

We had a family band called Nausea that would produce entire ad-libbed albums, created by recording backing tracks on a reel-to-reel tape machine and then adding overdubs by using a stereo tape machine to overlay parts. To this day, I find the process of recording music and overdubbing to feel magical, which goes back to these early, formative experiences.

The first concert I ever performed at was Anarchy in Steventon, a concert held in a hall within the village in the summer of 1977. It was organised by Dave Stevenson, the local vicar's son, to raise funds for the church roof. My brothers and neighbours played a three-hour set, which was disrupted by someone driving a moped into the hall and then a fight breaking out. Four London punks even turned up to the gig in the hope that the Dogends were actually the Sex Pistols playing under a pseudonym. I came on in the last half hour to play trombone on the Dogends song 'Back on My Heals Again'. I didn't want to leave the stage.

I played in a variety of bands in the early eighties, first off in Albert Park and His Playmates, then my best mate Will and I formed a three-piece with his friend Chris Hosegood called The Poles.

Will's parents were socialists and very, very liberal – quite a contrast from my home situation. His bedroom was a total mess, the floor littered with a riot of coins, newspapers, bottles of discarded piss, sheath knives, and plates with dried food encrusted on them. He had a succession of bongs, including a contraption that was coloured using crayons and named the 'psychedelic groove tube'. I can still recall the bitter-water taste in my mouth, and the length of cardboard from the inside of a kitchen roll and a pillow-full of smoke in my lungs. For even more psychotic smoking experiences, we would sit upside-down with our heads on a cushion and our legs balanced on the wall while someone blew smoke into our mouth. 'I feel like I am on another world with you'.

We would experiment with a variety of drugs in Will's bedroom, all the while tuning into albums like Magazine's *Secondhand Daylight* and *The Correct Use of Soap*, Jimi Hendrix's Capitol Records contractual obligation live album

*Band Of Gypsys*, The Animals' *Greatest Hits* and, of course, anything by The Only Ones, all played on Will's decrepit sixties radiogram.

In 1982, Will went off to university and I created a new outfit called Raise the Dust. We rehearsed in a barn in Sutton Courtenay, run by the people who would later manage Supergrass and Radiohead. We recorded at a 16-track studio in Milton, Oxfordshire, and did gigs locally and around London. I am convinced that we did a concert with Damon Albarn around 1983.

The first proper gig I went to was Ian Dury and The Blockheads, at the Oxford Apollo/New Theatre in 1978. I was bewitched by the whole evening. A local band called Ken Liversausage gave support and there was a raffle which culminated in an inflated rubber doll being donated to the winners and then thrown into the audience. The evening exploded when Ian Dury came on, limping around, saluting the audience with his larger-than-life Brel-esque stage personality, barking punk vocals against the tight funk and roll of The Blockheads. A handler came on and rearranged the motley collection of rags, scarves, bicycle bells and hooters attached to mic stands every time Dury discarded them or dropped them. His performance made it sexy to be different, to be disabled, to not give a fuck. It is often said that Ian Dury created the Vaudeville musical hall jumble sale template that John Lydon fed from in his transmutation into Johnny Rotten. The next morning I woke up wanting to be in The Blockheads.

In 1981, through a friend of my sister Vicky, I got a job working for a T-shirt bootlegger called Steve Vince. This was the first job I had in the music industry and it influenced how I would view it from that point on. Steve was a blagger – he ran a whole series of businesses with varying degrees of success. I'd sell T-shirts and button badges outside gigs.

During the Reading Festival that year, I sold bootlegged T-shirts with horrendous heavy metal logos. We would set up a makeshift stall outside a local's house – after paying them for the pitch – and stand there, encouraging folks to buy stuff. My spirit of performance came to the fore and I did quite well. I went home after that exhausting weekend with an almost unimaginable pay packet of 100 green pound notes in an envelope. Vicky grabbed all the notes and threw them up in the air, letting them all spill down across the bedroom like manna from heaven.

My first girlfriend was Tracy Simpson, she lived in Abingdon and attended my school, Larkmead, a bog-standard comprehensive. Our relationship began as the culmination of both of us appearing in starring roles in Bertolt Brecht's *The Threepenny Opera*, me as Macheath, or 'Mack the Knife', and her as Jenny. Tracy was not popular with my mother, who described her rather unfairly as a 'trainee Margaret Thatcher', but mothers are often withering about their precious sons' choice of mate. I lost my virginity to Tracy with The Doors' *Greatest Hits* as a soundtrack.

In 1983 I flunked my A levels and had to re-sit them. The following summer I went to stay with Tracy in West Berlin, where she was studying at the Berlin Free University. The flat Tracy and I stayed in was located in the largely Turkish inhabited neighbourhood of Neukölln, one of the hundreds of thousands of impersonal concrete tenements that must have mushroomed up in the sixties and seventies. It lacked a bathroom, so we would have to wash ourselves in the kitchen sink, a challenge that required a sense of balance, contortion and the ability to suspend a sense of the ridiculous.

My typical day would see me get up, get dressed, ride the U-Bahn to Kurfürstendamm, busk all day, then ride the U-Bahn back to Neukölln where we would spend all the money I had earned on food. The next day I would go out and do the same thing again. Whilst busking in Wittenbergplatz outside KaDeWe (Berlin's equivalent of Harrods) the staff in the music department got wise to the fact that I was the big-voiced nuisance who was polluting the sound of the streets, so they refused to sell me new guitar strings. I had to send in German punters to purchase them on my behalf.

It was a vibrant time to be visiting Berlin, which was still gripped by Cold War dissection. I felt a terrible sense of history, with the intimidating watchtowers still looking for Eastern escapees to shoot, and the central scrub in between the two states where once Hitler's bunker had been. The U-Bahn lines snaked through Western and Eastern sides of the city. The East German authorities closed all the stations that lay on their side of the border and sealed them up against their citizens. As a train came to the spot directly under the border, it passed through a concrete collar set in the roof and sides of the tunnel, through which the train only just fitted, thereby stopping anyone trying to escape by clinging to the outside of the coaches. The train would slow down through the darkened closed stations; in some places there were still advertising posters on the walls from 1961 when the Berlin Wall was first built. On the platforms strolled armed border guards who would glower at the well-dressed West Berliners on the train as it trundled by.

Somehow I forgot to extend my three-month ticket, and my brother Andrew had to come out and bring me home. When I arrived home I was given the job of picking redcurrants and blackcurrants from my mother's fruit bushes in the garden. I was so thin and hungry from my Berlin experience that I ate half of the fruit I was supposed to be collecting.

Once settled back in the UK, I prepared to begin my

BA Honours course in English Literature at Manchester Polytechnic. My school friends Raymond Breckon and Gordon MacKay also moved from Oxford to Manchester over that summer. In the spring of 1985, when Gordon convened a meeting at The Spinners pub in Hulme, we discussed forming the band that would become Too Much Texas.

# 3

## You're so shallow but you're in too deep

Too Much Texas started off as a three-piece: Gordon, Raymond and me, and a drum machine that Gordon would programme. Later, Bristolian drummer Chris Veale joined us. In the early days of Too Much Texas, we would rehearse in The Boardwalk on Little Peter Street, a disused school encompassing a cute old theatre with a stage in it, set before raised seats. The theatre and stage soon got ripped out as it became a proper live venue, and then later a club. Here we bashed out original compositions such as 'You've Got a Ticket To See James Dean', a bitchy song about some poly friends that had arranged a trip to see *East of Eden* in Hulme's community cinema, having neglected to invite either Kevin McCabe, my best friend at the college, or me.

We played at The Boardwalk, and someone must have liked us, because in the heady days that were indie music in 1985, we supported the likes of The Beloved, The House of Love and Ignition. Occasionally we would travel as far as London, Edinburgh or even Gloucester to do gigs.

Raymond and Gordon were quite pushy and were trying hard to make the band successful, especially after having located to a new city during the eighties recession. Gordon's girlfriend, Louise, made friends with a girl called Suzanne who ran the kitchen at the fairly recently opened Haçienda. Suzanne became our manager and the first thing she did was to get all of us jobs collecting glasses at the Haçienda, which meant that we were propelled into the very heart of creativity and madness that became the Manchester scene some years later.

Like the house in Frilford where I grew up, I can still walk round the Haçienda in my mind, knowing each step and turn of it intimately, having spent hundreds of hours walking round it, picking up empty glasses, negotiating with drunken and drugged punters over the last few microns of beer, wine or brandy.

Working at the Haçienda was a blast. I would arrive at the City Road Inn, a pub opposite the club, and have a pint while an atrocious duo would bash out 'popular' hits such as 'Delilah' and 'Summer Loving'. Then at 7:30pm I would walk through the black doors of the Haçienda. Being a student and singing in a band, money was in short supply and I used to find fifty pounds a month on the floor working there, dropped under tables, or around the can bar upstairs. Better in my student pocket.

Being a glass collector, or *pot collector* as the Northern lexicon would have it, was one of the best jobs you could have in the club. You were free to be admired by all the female club-goers, thirsty scholars didn't bully you at the bar, and you got plugged into the greatest, most eclectic jukebox in the world, ever. Disco, techno, house, hardcore, old soul records, new soul records, punk, indie, you name it. 'All And All' by Joyce Sims, 'Just Buggin' and 'Please Love Me' by Whistle, The SOS Band's 'Just Be Good To Me' – just the thought of those tunes puts flesh on my bones and gives me the shivers.

I remember thinking at the time that books, films and dramas would be written about the club. It was such a furnace of raw ideas and attitudes – the first truly super club in Europe in style, humour, self-importance and actual cultural importance. The splash it started still ripples throughout international global culture in TV, dance music, in our inner-city redevelopments, in our hopes, desires and diseases.

One of the funny things about the Haçienda is the media industry that has grown up around it after the event. I routinely see local celebrities pontificate on what it meant to be part of the club, and what is was like. I never saw the majority of these 'experts' there in the mid- to late-eighties – they are just airbrushing history, creating anachronisms like a clock in a Shakespeare play.

These were the relatively innocent days before the guns and the hype and the Madchester tourists. There were many distinct club nights at the Haçienda: the student night on a Thursday called Temperance, where The Smiths, The Buzzcocks and The Jesus and Mary Chain would get played by Dave Haslam; Mike Pickering and Graeme Park oversaw the Friday session called Nude Night, where soul and house transformed the dance floor into a big drug church; the Saturday night was an explosive dance night, and once a month there was a gay night called Flesh on a Wednesday.

Brendon and Glenn were the couple who ran the Gay Traitor bar in the basement of the club. It is often forgotten by the 'new' Haçienda 'experts', that it was very much a gay club. We forget that having such a high profile, gay-friendly space was actually very progressive of Manchester in the eighties. This, along with the revolutions of music, drugs and sex, is why the Haçienda was the ground zero of its day. Not just flares, T-shirts and glow sticks – thank Christ!

I saw quite a selection of bands perform at the Haçienda when I worked there. The Alarm gig was a sell-out, but quite odd with a lot of hair. Happy Mondays played in 1987, and I went because Terry Hall said that they were the best new band in Britain. All the way through their set, they looked as though they were going to kick the shit out of the entire audience – boys, girls, cripples, pets, the lot.

They were fantastic, with their mix of industrial funk punk scatter. Watching The Residents made you feel as if you were hallucinating and the top of your head was coming off. Peter Tosh was great, but Ghost Dance were a little too goth for my taste, not really my cup of tea. I remember Frankie Goes to Hollywood's Paul Rutherford and Holly Johnson arriving on stage, driving up a ramp on enormous motorbikes. I didn't see every band, sadly, missing the likes of Divine, Madonna and The Stone Roses.

The bar staff would work six hours a night, finishing at two o'clock – no all-night licences for us. At the end of the night we would have a drink on the house and crack jokes. That made the night special, to be sat in the club with the lights on, talking and smoking and enjoying the inside track. A lot of wonderful folk worked at the Haçienda, including Leroy Johnson, the bar manager, who was a very funny and wise man. Marcia was a beautiful black lady who worked in the cloakroom, a really sassy earth-mother type who had a lovely low laugh. Paul Cons, the event manager, had a big red Afro which tapered around the back of his head like a pair of buttocks, earning him the nickname 'Bumhead'. Paul Mason was the bespectacled manager who was brought in by Factory around 1986 to try to make the club operate on a greater business footing. Of course he was pretty much despised by the rump of people who worked there. The task of even attempting to make the club operate on a business footing was as easy as nailing jelly to a wall. Decent, talented local people needed to be respected and, memorably, Paul got thumped outside the club during the Festival of the Tenth Summer because he wouldn't let Derek Johnson into the gig.

Occasionally, after hours, some of the staff would go with Leroy to the Reno, a black club on Princess Road in Moss Side. We used to go down to the dank cellar, which was full to the brim with African-Caribbean revellers. It seemed as though all their community were there: saints, soldiers, prophets, gangsters, young girls, mothers, brothers, uncles, mad men, drunks, drug addicts and ravers. It was as if no one was left on the outside, everyone had their place and was protected from the harsh realities of the racist, raining Britain outside. The music was a mix of reggae, dancehall, lovers rock, soft sweet soul and dance music.

Many people involved in the television/music/ entertainment business would turn up after the clubs in town had shut. It's where Tony Wilson would take fawning American record executives when negotiating deals. How much he must have enjoyed witnessing their unease and alienation, and how this levelling of matters must have made his acolytes swiftly accede to whatever business advantage he was pursuing. One night a fight broke out and swept through the cellar like a tsunami. A sea of fists connecting with skin and bone. Leroy, anticipating danger as only a natural bar manager and roadie can, pulled us out of harm's way with one pluck of his powerful grip.

The last time we visited the Reno, Leroy warned us bar staff to stand with our backs to the wall while queuing up to get in. We followed his advice unswervingly. Only a month later, a white club-goer got stabbed in the back waiting to gain entrance to the club: he stumbled a hundred yards up to an unmanned police station and died there. The Council's response was to announce that the road was being widened, a piece of local planning that no one in the area had previously been aware of. The JCBs and wrecking balls descended and the whole institution that had been there for years was gone within half an hour. One effect that the demolition of the Reno had was to accelerate and encourage the growth of gang wars in Manchester, as it deprived the black community of a bolt-hole, a secure place that was their own. There is a lot to be said for communities that look after themselves.

I was living in Hulme, a concrete mess built in the sixties, including five crescent-shaped flats ironically named after famous architects from the preceding three centuries, hence Robert Adam Crescent, William Kent Crescent and so on. It looked like five spaceships had landed and been left abandoned. There was a pub in the middle of the crescents called The White Horse, where bands of the time such as King Kurt, Big Flame, Twang, Dub Sex, Tools You Can Trust, and Inca Babies used to drink. One night I went there to meet a girl called Alison (a neighbour of Raymond from Too Much Texas) to see if she could mend a jacket that I had just bought from Affleck's Palace and that was already falling to bits. I went back to her flat, we drank a bottle of vodka and I ended up living with her for the next thirteen years.

Alison ran an independent women's club-wear label called Baylis and Knight, which was initially based at her Hulme flat. When I met Alison, she had a two-and-a-half-year-old daughter called Holly. There was a smack dealer living four doors down, and people would be shouting at him all hours, so that they could throw some money up to his balcony in order for him to throw a bag of heroin down. Eventually, a rival 'business' broke into his flat and he had to throw himself twenty feet off his balcony onto the deck access pathway to escape.

There was a family of thrushes that made their nest up above the front door of 321 Robert Adam Crescent. The mother would dive-bomb you, protecting her chicks, every time you tried to get in the flat. I was impressed that the baby birds could go from hatching to flying in about two-and-a-half weeks, when it takes humans fifteen years just to look after themselves. Eventually, Alison and I planned to fly this coup too.

In 1986 we moved her business out of the flat and into a workroom in town on Bloom Street, and then to a 200-square metre workroom on Sackville Street. We decided to live in the workroom over the winter months, as it featured heating that was included in the rental price. Living in this attractive loft space wasn't officially allowed, so we had a fold-down bed in case the landlord or health and safety officials turned up. Holly had a makeshift bedroom, made with paper walls which stretched from the floor to the twenty-foot high ceiling. It was a bit like living in The Beatles' house in the film *Help*, a secret massive open-plan living space, and a double interior/exterior life. The 200-square metre space was rented at a cost of £15 a week.

Around this time, Suzanne got Too Much Texas a support slot for New Order at the Haçienda and we spat and shouted our way through a twenty-two minute set, which seemed to last a lifetime while we were playing it. Peter Hook's bass amps seemed bigger than the pyramids. We also recorded a track that was released as a flexi disc on Dave Haslam's fanzine, *Debris*. The song was called 'Fixed Link', and was a Gang of Four-esque ditty dedicated to the channel tunnel, which Margaret Thatcher had just given the green light to. On the same flexi disc was another band called Soil. John Peel was going to play the Soil track on the radio but the track skipped when Peel tried to play it, so he played ours instead.

Raymond pushily rang up BBC radio that night – he had obtained the reception number from directory enquiries. John Peel just happened to be passing the phone as it rang. Raymond explained who he was, and cheekily asked if we could do a session. One was immediately booked.

We recorded our debut single at Square One in Bury. It was engineered by Tom Oliver, a friend of Suzanne's who had recorded stuff for Kalima, a jazz band on Factory. The tape operator for this debut single was a fifteen-year-old on work experience called Damon Gough. The single was self-financed, but we persuaded Guy Lovelady, a local music fan, to put it out on his Ugly Man label. We got reviews in the polytechnic's *Pulp* newspaper and in *The Word*, which was the pop page of the *Manchester Evening News*.

In the summer of 1988 I decided that Too Much Texas couldn't self-finance another single. We needed someone to at least pay for the pressing and the promotion, even if we were still required to pay for the recording. I found myself flicking through the shelves of Piccadilly Records and as I looked in the indie section I found 'Plane Crash', the debut 7-inch single by Inspiral Carpets. My only previous experience of them had been to see their track 'Garage Full of Flowers' on a flexi disc, given away with another edition of *Debris* fanzine. I copied down the address of Playtime Records from the back of the single and set off to the second-floor office on Princess Street, where I met Paula Greenwood, impresario of Playtime. I gave Paula a demo of the recordings of our new material. Luckily, she liked my voice and the songs.

Paula was always a bit of an enigma. You couldn't tell if she was gay, bisexual, or straight. However, our music touched her and turned her on, that was evident from this first meeting. My voice had form for touching people. Guy Lovelady once said that listening to me singing was like 'copping off with a girl', which raised some eyebrows amongst the Too Much Texas camp.

Like the Ugly Man label, Playtime had a production and distribution deal with the independent record wholesaler Red Rhino, but just as we began discussing with Paula the release of our *Volcano* EP, Red Rhino went bust, leaving Paula and Playtime with no money back from the records sold, and no new way of accessing production or distribution. Paula had a bevy of other artists on her record label roster, including Inspiral Carpets, Mirrors Over Kiev, and New Fast

Automatic Daffodils. At this time Inspiral Carpets were the only band on the label that any other distribution company wanted to sign.

Paula's plan was to get Too Much Texas out supporting Inspirals until a new production and distribution deal could be struck. Between late summer and winter 1988, Too Much Texas supported Inspiral Carpets at Hull Adelphi and ULU in London.

Inspirals had started to become a force to be reckoned with. They were featured highly in Peel's Festive Fifty, at No. 11 with 'Keep The Circle Around'. The Festive Fifty was a chart of all the year's favourite releases voted on by Peel's devoted fans, which went out as a show, with all the featured tracks played in reverse order at New Year. The Inspirals had cemented a firm following of fans all over the UK and beyond, via gigs and records, fanzines, press interviews and reviews. They were powerful, like a Northern Stranglers. They were lyrical and melodic in a way that contemporaries like The Wedding Present could never be.

After months of meetings with Paula, two separate things happened. The first was that a distributor called Nine Mile, who had risen phoenix-like from the ashes of Red Rhino, found the home phone numbers of the Inspirals and started trying to do a deal with them without Paula and Playtime. The second thing was that Inspiral Carpets imploded.

Bass player Dave Swift left Inspirals in the autumn of 1988 to pursue a full-time computer course. Martyn Walsh was recruited from local support act, The Next Step. The Inspirals did one last concert with this temporary line-up in London, and then the singer Stephen Holt left the band. I have never really found out why Stephen left, but I think it was a combination of factors. Inspiral Carpets was started by Graham Lambert in 1982 as a bedroom band called The Furs who played The Psychedelic Furs covers. Stephen Holt was a long-time friend of Graham's. Clint Boon ran a rehearsal space in Ashton-under-Lyne called The Mill. In the daytime he manufactured furniture, and by night he recorded bands on his 4-track. One day Clint simply picked up his Farfisa keyboard and plonked it in the rehearsal room while Inspirals were playing, so he allegedly never actually officially joined the band. I think that a power struggle ensued; that there were disagreements between the parties about how to deal with the Playtime/Red Rhino debacle; and that Stephen issued Graham and the band an ultimatum: 'It's me or Clint.'

Whatever caused Inspiral Carpets to fracture at this point, they were left with a series of problems. They had recorded a new EP, *Trainsurfing*, which would have been released in the summer of 1988 if Playtime had a distributor. They had built up a head of steam by being a great band, playing a lot of shows, and by being lovely, funny, rude people. It would have been a shame to lose all that momentum by failing to find a replacement lead singer. Clint momentarily tried out as front man, but it just didn't work, it detracted from his Farfisa keyboard duties, so a singer had to be found.

Auditions began after Stephen Holt left. Famously, Noel Gallagher tried out on the evening of the Lockerbie bombing, 21st December 1988. He had a go at singing the Inspirals song 'Whiskey', but found the lyrics to be too daft, and this didn't go down well. Two other singers tried out – one was John Matthews from the band Turning Blue. I don't know the name of the other singer – I think it was a friend of Martyn Walsh's, but none of them were any bloody good. Inspirals had enjoyed watching Too Much Texas supporting them at the three or so shows we did together, and I think that Graham and Clint liked my powerful, no-nonsense singing.

So came the evening of 20th February 1989 when Binsey Smith rang me and asked if I wanted to audition for the band, four hours before they were to perform an instrumental version of 'Directing Traffic' on Tony Wilson's TV show, *The Other Side of Midnight*. The next day I went to see Gordon and Raymond from Too Much Texas to tell them that I was auditioning with Inspiral Carpets. I said to them that, even if I didn't pass the audition, things were probably up for Too Much Texas. I didn't want to fuck things up by not being straight with my old school mates.

The first show I did with Inspiral Carpets was at Middlesex Polytechnic on 2nd March 1989. I was inexperienced at singing in the band, still filling a dead man's shoes so to speak. Later, on that first *Trainsurfing* tour, we played an old cinema in Northampton which had been converted into a venue called The Electra. I went out through a set of fire doors which closed behind me and left me stuck, locked in a tiny space between two sets of doors, in limbo, a perfect image for where I was in my life; the past shut to me and the future unsure as well. I began the concert staring out at the audience in a disconnected way.

# 4

## You've got 27 years on me

My first tour with the Inspirals culminated in a triumphant sold-out homecoming gig at The Boardwalk. I embarrassed the band's cool by overreacting to the heroes' welcome; I wasn't used to such receptions back in the Too Much Texas or Poles days. I mouthed 'We Love You' to the crowd at the end of the gig and was lampooned for it for weeks after by Craig, Clint and Graham impersonating my lisping Southern accent: 'We Looovee Yoouu'.

We'd sometimes be working seven-day weeks, driving up to gigs in Scotland or down to Wales, and then having to drive back the same night to the dusty paint-ridden air of The Mill where we would unpack all the equipment, and then be dropped off home, one by one. As with all groups, a massive over importance is attached to the order in which band members are dropped off. The order usually reflects the level of importance that band members consider themselves to be. Our pecking order was also influenced by whether the band member lived in North or South Manchester. We used to joke that the band would have split up before Manchester's new circular motorway was completed. This is, of course, exactly what happened.

It is a given that, in any tight-knit cluster of workers, be they brickies, carpet fitters, politicians, fishermen, surgeons or Oxford academics, they will organise themselves into well-wrought established hierarchies within the group. These pecking orders are endlessly questioned, re-negotiated and re-affirmed. Bands are families.

Clint was the father. It is clear that, from the moment that Stephen Holt had been pushed or had jumped or whatever, Clint was the undisputed star of the band. I love the man, but here it is out in the open: Clint was the dad. If Clint was the dad then Graham, the founder, was the mother of the band. The history of Inspiral Carpets is, in a strange way, the history of Graham.

When Craig joined, he was the baby of the band. He originally met them when they were playing a Saturday afternoon gig in Oldham. Chris Goodwin, their drummer at the time, had failed to turn up. Inspirals decided to do the concert without him at which point Dougie, Craig's dad, suggested that his fourteen-year-old son could come and play. Craig did the gig and has been with Inspirals ever since. He literally grew up in the band. He was once given detention by a teacher who disbelieved the truthful explanation that his previous day's absence from school had been caused by playing a concert in Camden.

Martyn Walsh was the shy bass player from Denton, the same town as Mick Hucknall and Mark Reeder. Martyn was naturally shy, but very smart and funny, in a more considered, satirical way than the Oldham contingent. I was bottom of the pile, last one in, etcetera, etcetera. Perhaps it was because I was the youngest of seven and always felt the need to fit in, but I never really felt that Inspiral Carpets was *my* band in the way that Too Much Texas had been.

In the heady days of 1989 we had a variety of folk working for us, including Noel Gallagher. Noel was in his early twenties then and was a very smart, funny, street urchin; a bit like the Artful Dodger from *Oliver Twist*. He tried to start things off on a good footing with me by saying that he liked Too Much Texas' 'Fixed Link', the *Debris* flexi disc track that we had released.

At this point, I didn't know anything about Noel's audition

– that was kept from me in a conspiracy of silence by all of the other band members until some three years later – but I presume I must have been the epitome of a lot of things Noel would have despised: a lisping middle-class southerner and the one who got the job that he wanted. Noel and me started off being so at odds with each other that things could only get better.

Noel was very shy yet immensely piss-taking, and he fulfilled the role within the band of roadie, confidant, joker, sounding board and sage. Noel's triangulation within the band was a complicated one because now, not only did I have to put up with the bullying of the other band members vying for supposed supremacy, but I also had to contend with the people working for us taking the piss. Band members used Noel's envy and grievances as a launch pad to attack other band members: what a lovely soup to find oneself in!

Noel came along to roadie on a couple of gigs in early 1989; he couldn't always make weekday gigs, as he and his brothers, Paul and Liam, worked for their dad's building company, digging drains for British Gas. In the summer of 1989, Noel suffered an accident while at work, when a steel cap from a gas pipe fell on his right foot and crushed it. He was unable to work, so he came on the road with Inspirals while his foot – in plaster – mended. He never went back to digging drains for gas pipes.

A significant event for the future of Manchester music had been the Anti Clause 28 concert at the International 2 venue on Plymouth Grove on 30th May 1988. A lot of relationships were made that night. It was before I had met Inspirals, but Clint and Craig and Graham were there and it's where Graham met Noel for the first time. Alison and I went to the concert because James were playing. Word had it that The Stone Roses were playing too.

Between 1986 and 1987 Too Much Texas had regularly rehearsed next to The Stone Roses in a practice room in Chorlton, near the Feathers pub, with the vibrations seeping through the walls. We used a roadie of theirs to drive us to Too Much Texas gigs – a lad called Paul, who had no teeth, and was a part-time cross-dresser. I occasionally saw him, in all his finery, frequenting B&Q looking for hammers and screws. I had seen Ian Brown hanging out in the Haçienda when I had worked there a few years previously and I knew that Mani went out with Lisa, one of the DJs from The Boardwalk. Mani used to play in a band with Clint called T'Mill back in The Mill at Oldham.

The Stone Roses kept the sell-out audience waiting that night, and didn't come on stage until 12.15am, at which point the room was electric: Reni, behind his paint-splattered drum kit, dwarfing it as he sang his heart out, hat balanced uphill on his head; Ian Brown, smashing the microphone stand, and spouting ambiguous rants at the stalls, making it obvious that they weren't there for the cause, they were there for the music; and Mani and John, pounding their bass and electric guitars. The songs exploded round the venue – 'Waterfall', 'She Bangs the Drums'… It was punk, it was electric, it started a revolution.

This 1988 show created a universal language of excitement about The Stone Roses, about what was possible and what could happen. It was consciousness-raising to say the least and would feed directly into what Inspiral Carpets would do over the following years.

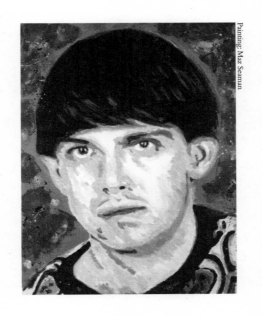

## II

## *Life*

# 5

## Please be cruel

One morning in London, I was being driven along in a minibus with Graham, Craig and Noel. In front of us in the stop-start traffic was a Luton van, with its back shutter open. In the back of this van were several large free-standing electric fans. After a few minutes of being in standing traffic, the bored conversation turned to Craig challenging Noel to steal one of the fans, saying that it was just what he needed to keep him cool at gigs under the lights whilst drumming. After about three seconds of goading, Noel leapt out of our minibus and, unseen by the delivery driver, jumped up onto the back of the van. Just at that moment, the traffic in front sped off and Noel, who had just fixed his hands on one of the fans, lost his balance and fell backwards. We were in fits of laughter as Noel, van and fans sped off into the distance and through a set of lights which turned red and halted our pursuit. Eventually we caught up with the van a mile up the road and Noel scrambled back towards us with the prize in his hands. A 'snapper-up of unconsidered trifles' as Autolycus from Shakespeare's *Winter's Tale* would have it.

It's a badly kept secret that most bands on the way to fame and fortune behave like arseholes. As you ascend the rock and rollercoaster, it becomes easy to turn fairly unpleasant along the way – as the youthful feeling of being indestructible and the adulation of fans kick in. Robbing and smashing up dressing rooms became the flavour of 1989. Holed up in a student union office somewhere in the Midlands, where they'd idiotically housed us in the Ents Officer's room, Craig destroyed a typewriter by hitting the keys violently and rhythmically with a hammer, while another band member pissed in a filing cabinet and Clint stole a rather pleasing picture of Daleks trundling over London Bridge. God, these promoters were trusting. We played a club situated in the middle of the Birmingham Police Headquarters and helped ourselves to beers and mixers — I mean who is going to expect someone to tan a club in the middle of a police station? In Bangor someone stole the DJ's records and after the show we gave the very same DJ a lift in our van. Unbeknownst to him, he was actually perched on top of his own record collection. Bad karma.

We played at the Citadel in St Helens and some fool gave us the in-house art gallery as a dressing room. Along the four walls of the rectangular gallery were a collection of fairly amateur portraits — still lifes of unrealistic fruit, vegetables and dogs. Each painting had a title, a pretentious description of the material it was made from, and an extortionate price, such as 'The Dog, acrylic paint on canvas, £80.' First, we decided to swap all the pictures round so that the one of the marrow had the sign saying it was a dog etc. Not content with this level of sabotage, Clint then used his art-school polished cartoon drawing to mock each picture by drawing a satirical one which we then put up behind the proper one: 'Two Dogs Fucking! medium permanent marker pen on paper, £90!' We found a painting which had a real tie attached to the neck of a portrait and Graham snipped the end of the tie off with a pair of scissors, Morecambe and Wise style. Later, when the poor woman who had entrusted us with the room complained that a portion of the tie was missing, Graham held the small bit of cloth up to her face and said, 'No, it's not missing, it's here!' While all of this was going on, in the audience was local musician

Richard Ashcroft, who cites this show as being the first gig he ever attended.

Our booking agent in the early days of 1989 was Sean Johnson at the Miracle Music agency. He had been a fantastic help at the start, but we had quickly outgrown him. When recording and mixing tracks for our first album, *Life*, Sean kept on booking us gigs where the fee didn't reflect our new-found star indie status. He booked us to play a gig at Loughborough University as part of an anti-Poll Tax event, for a fee of just £50. Another gig was at the Goldsmiths Tavern in London for the Entertainment Officer's twenty-first birthday. Again the fee was a tiny £50 – not a lot for a band that had three songs in the indie top thirty at the same time. When we turned up at the gig, there were only six people in the audience.*

The final straw was a concert in Blackburn at a northern soul venue called the Cellar Vie club. We were recording in the studio, so dismantling the drum kit and losing the microphone placings would cost us more in money and time than the £100 fee that the gig was fetching. We called Sean and asked him, very nicely, to cancel the gig. He bravely responded by giving the promoter our studio phone number. We began to get phone calls every hour or so from him, who, keen not to lose a profitable show, employed reverse psychology. During one phone call he said, 'So you're too scared to play in Blackburn, are you?'

Of course we did the show, but when we turned up we saw that the support band had brought baseball bats. The northern soulers in the corner initially despised us, and didn't like their club being taken over by Oldham wags. All this

*Five years later, Damon Albarn explained to me that the Entertainment Officer was their first manager, and that the six punters were actually the pre-Blur band, Seymour. Damon said that we had played the concert as if there were an audience of thousands.

was a little ironic, as the gig had been booked without our prior knowledge or any desire on our behalf to do it, but it somehow turned out to be a good gig after all. It's always a pleasurable challenge to win people over at a gig.

We eventually got shot of Sean by inviting his boss, Steve Parker, to our office on Sackville Street and surreptitiously recorded the meeting on a cassette Walkman. Our manager, Binsey, had foolishly signed an exclusive agency contract with Miracle. It is fairly standard music industry protocol to never sign exclusively with a live agent, so that you are free to go elsewhere if they mess up negotiating on your behalf. Binsey, in his naivety, had signed the agency contract giving Miracle exclusive right to book our shows worldwide. However, the band had the foresight to include a key-man clause, which meant that if Sean Johnson went to another agency, we could go with him and, furthermore, would be freed from the existing signed agency contract.

Sean's boss, Steve, agreed that Sean wasn't up to the job and would let him go. Of course, this was all on tape. We then informed Steve that as Sean was no longer working for Miracle we were now released from the exclusive agency contract. It was a subtle way to get out of it.

Driven and career-minded as we were in these matters, it is often the ability of artists to be bloody-minded, and to push beyond others, that leads to success. Around this time we played a sell-out gig in Birmingham where we came up with a scheme to charge people in through the fire door at the back of the venue – we made about £60, which was a fortune to five working lads who paid themselves just £15 a week.

We formed our own label, Cow Records, in March 1989. We initially set the label up with assistance from Eastern Bloc, a thriving record shop based in the Arcade, behind Affleck's

Palace. They had a production and distribution deal with Nine Mile, and could provide us with some good contacts because they were running their own label, Creed, which had 808 State.

The *Trainsurfing* EP was released through Cow/Creed. Although we were supposed to put the whole pressing of a thousand 12-inch singles through Nine Mile's national distribution system, what we actually did was autograph 50% of the initial pressing, which Eastern Bloc then sold on to other shops in the North and Scotland for an increased price. We signed all 500 of them in Eastern Bloc's horrible sewage-smelling cellar stockroom under the shop, and they gave us a free album in return. The record was a success, the initial pressing sold out and was re-pressed.

In 1989 we released *Trainsurfing* in March; then the singles 'Joe' in April, 'Find Out Why' in June and 'Move' in July. Each record was doing better than the last, selling exponentially twice the preceding release. A standard question at gigs from punters and in interviews was: 'When's *Plane Crash* coming out?' This EP featured Stephen Holt on vocals. At first we had wanted to re-release it, but as the momentum of the new line-up and positive vibe kicked in, we decided not to because it was time to cement the new line-up in the record-buying public's mind. I always felt that Steve's versions of those early songs were better than my later versions, so had no problem with the EP going out. In fact, given that there was demand for *Plane Crash*, I convinced the band to put it out as a bootleg. My theory was one rooted firmly in the Malcolm McLaren/Colonel Tom Parker school of rock management – there is no point in getting upset by the old singer's singing when you can make a bit of money from it. We pressed up 2000 copies and sold them through the classified adverts of the *NME*.

The first single that featured me on vocals, 'Joe', was

recorded at Square One and produced by 808 State's Graham Massey and Martin Price. While we were in the studio, Pricey and the band started writing stupid stuff all over the mixing-desk using a chinagraph pencil. Pricey would write 'Sound as Fuck', and one of the band would up the ante by writing 'Safe as Fuck', and eventually 'Cool as Fuck', and a phrase was born. We started saying it all the time, and pretty soon we put it on a T-shirt.

One of the key reasons the Inspiral Carpets ended up being successful was our sheer bloody cheek. We built up such a head of steam that, without any investment, expensive video and press budgets, or the help of a management or record company promotional department, we managed to get to No. 49 with 'Move' in the UK singles chart.

I sometimes get sent questionnaires from PhD students reading at American universities who are writing about the cultural implications of the Manchester scene as represented by The Stone Roses, Happy Mondays and Inspiral Carpets. They quiz me about Factory records and often assume that Inspiral Carpets would have loved to have signed a recording contract with Factory, when in reality the truth couldn't have been more different.

My experiences of working at the Haçienda taught me that the central core of Factory – Tony Wilson, Rob Gretton, Alan Wise and Mike Pickering – were good, funny, interesting people, but smart, professional, business people they were not. At the outset of house music, the Haçienda played host to obscure records that weren't licensed in the UK for distribution and release. A prime example is 'Ride on Time' by Black Box, the famous club record which featured illegally sampled vocals by Loretta Holloway. Mike Pickering played that record for a year when he was the only person in the UK who actually owned a copy. Factory could have licensed that record, and any other number that its DJs were regularly playing, for peanuts and could have made a fortune, but Factory, being Factory, with its heady mixture of aesthetics, bluff and incompetence, refused or failed to exploit the position it had as Europe's first super club. Mike Pickering eventually had to set up his own Deconstruction label to sign the records that Factory wouldn't sign.

Rather than signing to Factory, we just found out who was doing the plugging for the Mondays and employed them independently. Jeff Barrett and Jayne Houghton did our press with Nicki Kefalas from Out Promotions taking care of radio and TV.

Jeff Barrett was riotously funny and worked out of an office on Clerkenwell Road in London. He was in the same building as Creation, and did press for Primal Scream. He was setting up his label, Heavenly, at that time, and had a label deal with London Records. He had just signed a young Welsh band called Manic Street Preachers. London Records were making a mess of his label deal, so Jeff managed to get the band released in order that they could sign to Columbia Records instead.

Jayne Houghton really did a lot of the day-to-day national press, organising interviews and reviews with the *NME*, *Melody Maker* and *Sounds*. We stayed at Jayne's house in London because we were skint and had been invited to record a Peel session when another band pulled out at the last minute. While we were at Jayne's house, someone tried to steal her scooter but he was spotted by Graham and Craig, who ran out after him in their underpants. Lord knows what the prospective thief must have thought of having two near-naked Oldhamers chasing after him in the early hours of the morning. Of course, Jayne restaged the heroic have-a-go heroes in the *NME* the following week.

We went from being a relatively unknown band when I joined in February 1989 to holding impressive recording and publishing deals by January 1990, quite an achievement for a bunch of lads that Shaun Ryder had branded 'clueless knobheads'. In 1989, Binsey and I met the Mondays' manager Nathan McGough and Shaun Ryder in a London bank. They were laughing at Binsey's enormous mobile phone, which took two hands to carry. They weren't laughing a few months later when we had out-manoeuvred their band as the result of clever management and the ability to be contacted anywhere at any time.

In early 1989 we left Playtime Records and the process of shopping for a record deal was a complex one. John Bryce from CBS was a tireless supporter of Inspirals and did his level best to sign us. He is a great person, however we felt that his colleagues at CBS were lawyer-types, and we didn't feel confident that they really wanted Inspiral Carpets – it felt as though they just wanted to make a quick buck by putting out the first album and then dropping us once the Manchester fashion had moved on. They offered us £200,000 and a 14% percentage artist royalty, which meant that we would only make £14 from each £100 profit they made. This was a typical 'major' type deal.

Between ourselves we secretly discounted CBS as being the correct label for Inspiral Carpets, but we didn't advertise this decision or externally remove them from the running, as it was flattering to have such a big label give chase, and it also gave us leverage when talking to other potential bidders. Interestingly, CBS eventually gave 'our' deal to the wonderful The Real People in 1990, who they signed for one album and then dropped.

We then went to see Chrysalis Records, when the only artists of note on their roster were Debbie Harry and Billy Idol. The actual A&R scout was called Craig, and he was switched on and the genuine article, but the rest of the staff were a bit hopeless. In our initial meeting with them they got the name of our band and label wrong. We'd heard a rumour that they had signed a Liverpudlian band called The Rain who they seemed to think were The Real People. They signed them for £200,000, released a totally unsuccessful record, and then dropped them. Did we really want to instruct our musical careers to these people in return for £200,000?

We also talked to Zomba Records about a publishing and record deal. We were a little wary of them because they were a South African Company who controlled Silvertone, the tiny imprint that industry veteran Andrew Lauder ran and signed The Stone Roses to. With Zomba, we felt at the back of our minds that in offering us a deal, they might be signing up the competition to close us down, a business practice that goes on all over the economy, and not one we wanted to experience. The two A&R men who came to see us were like characters from the TV programme *Minder* – one would only ever say, in bright stage-school cockney, 'Alright mate!' The other, a prospective Arthur Daley, was the sort that would try to get us to sign a forty-six-page, thirteen album deal, backstage and without a lawyer present. Yeah, right – how many previous owners?

Brian Eno's EG label expressed an interest in signing us, but we didn't feel it had the size to handle the sales we could achieve in 1990, although we loved the idea of being on his imprint. We talked to ex-Stiff supremo Dave Robinson, who had Les Négresses Vertes signed to his new label, but we felt he had too many scores to settle with the rest of the music industry to hitch ourselves up to his wagon.

In the end, we negotiated a record deal with Mute in November 1989 for an advance of £60,000 and a 50/50 profit-share deal on royalties. As far as their business affairs people were concerned, Mute were laying out a lot of capital in signing the band and wanted to make sure we were an insurable risk. They insisted that we all had HIV tests. Off we all bumbled to a clinic in Didsbury where we gave blood samples, then heard nothing for months. Eventually Binsey informed us that we were all HIV negative. Clint responded to this news by grabbing hold of a fire escape rope in the first floor window of the studio and jumping out with a loud 'Yippee'.

After we signed with Mute, we decided that the partitioned office space in Sackville Street wasn't swanky enough, so we moved across town to an office space in Shudehill, a building called 23 New Mount Street. So posh was the general atmosphere of the new Cow Records office that even our American agent, Marc Geiger from the William Morris Agency in LA, couldn't believe the sophistication.

Clint's girlfriend, Debbie Black, had been the band's continual companion in these early days. During the mid- to late-eighties Clint and Debbie were virtually inseparable – wherever Clint went, she followed. As we began to become nationally successful, the rest of us felt that it wasn't strictly fair having one of the band member's partner with us, while the rest of us were away from our girlfriends most of the time. It was therefore decided that Debbie should run our office. The process of separating Debbie from Clint was one which ended with them ultimately splitting up.

Debbie left her job in order to work full-time with Binsey in the office. Debbie was a great office manager, she was quietly determined, and would always protect Clint's, and ultimately our, position. She was the point of contact for our fans, the trusted link in the chain passing information between the band and its followers.

# 6

## You should learn to walk before you crawl

All that wonderful year of 1989 we spent driving around in vans, listening to a mixture of music including De La Soul's *3 Feet High and Rising*; cassettes recorded from Piccadilly Radio's Saturday night dance show; The Stone Roses; and especially the song 'Back to Life' by Soul II Soul from their debut album *Club Classics, Vol. One*. And that was where, at Craig's suggestion, we got the title for our own debut album.

The *Life* album began as a collection of singles, which we recorded and released independently on our Cow label throughout 1989. Once 'Joe' had been recorded and released, we decided that we wanted to record future material with Nick Garside, so we moved from the dusty old mill in Ashton, into the Out of the Blue rehearsal room on Blossom Street. Nick had a small terrier called Max, and frequently he would be heard to shout, in a camp nasal inflection, 'Max, oh for God's sake, Max.' This became a bit of an in-joke and Clint, a keen impersonator, would ring Nick and open the phone call in a 'Nick' voice saying, 'Hi Nick, it's Nick here. Oh, for God's sake Max, stop messing around!'

The rehearsal room was also a recording studio. Comprising of a series of workrooms, formerly used as sweatshops in the 19th and 20th centuries, the complex was run by Nick and his friend Adam. Bands such as Yargo, James, 808 State and the folk-punk band To Hell With Burgundy used to rehearse there.

Word had it that back in the early eighties, an inception

of the band that went on to become The Smiths rehearsed there too. Adjacent to the rehearsal room was a pub that the local postal workers used to drink in called The Smiths Arms. On the walls of the lounge bar were front pages from the *Daily Record* recounting memorable days at the end of the Second World War, including D–Day and VE Day. One had the headline 'Louder than Bombs' emblazoned on it. We will possibly never know if The Smiths got their band name from the pub, and the name of one of their albums from a headline displayed within, but it would seem strange if the two things didn't have at least some influence upon them.

Nick Garside was working simultaneously on our debut album and James' *Gold Mother* record. Tim Booth always maintained that we had filched the verse for 'This Is How It Feels' from the James song 'Black Hole', although I can't hear it myself. That said, working in that creative nexus, we definitely sucked up some of the creative rhythms of Yargo, who rehearsed next door to us. You can hear the influence of their stripped-down reggae, funk influence in the bass and drums of our song 'Sackville', which closes the second side of the album.

The album starts with a submarine-like noise played on the lower keys of Clint's trusty Farfisa. The idea was that it would sound like one of the thousands of house records that we had all heard spilling out across the vast terrain of the Haçienda's expansive dance floor. Then, forty seconds into the song, the guitar, bass and drum kit explode into life. Once the band join in, impressive flourishes on the Farfisa kick in, introducing a fast, punky vocal to that first song, 'Real Thing'.

## Real Thing

This song was a group composition, with Martyn writing some of the basic chord progression and chorus lyrics. I wrote the verse lyrics, and Clint, Graham and Craig stitched the arrangement together. It encapsulates many of the common themes of songs written or co-written by Martyn, where the central 'voice' in the song is violently raging against unrequited love, sexual desire and jealousy, all swirling around in their own Inspiral galaxy. We regularly opened gigs with this song.

## Song For A Family

This song couldn't be more different from its predecessor. Lyrically and melodically, it borrows some influence from the ponderous depths of Echo & the Bunnymen's 'Read It In Books'. The stop-start rhythm of the song hangs around a back-feel bass line, a snaggling guitar part, and an almost reggae-feel recurring drum riff. Lyrically, Clint was presenting a realist, Northern, working-class picture: the music of the terraces, the turnstiles, the launderette and the pub, where the natural dignity of the working man is set against the human ability to dream of going beyond the honesty of the every day. These were themes that we would hear recurring in Clint's lyrics over each of the four albums that we recorded.

## This Is How It Feels

Clint brought the words and the music into the rehearsal room at Out of the Blue, and we played through it. The song was the first one in the Manchester era that, to my mind, wasn't just about hedonism. It stood up for the small voice, the misunderstood, the under-represented – a position that we could appreciate as the third band in the Manchester movement. Unfortunately, others who were less inspired took from our inspiration and, within six months, the Liverpudlian Farm had garnered Pachelbel's Canon to the mawkish lyric about Germans and Scousers in the trenches on Christmas day that is 'All Together Now'. Frequently, when I talk to punters about Inspiral Carpets they say, 'Didn't you record "All Together Now"?' when they really mean 'This Is How It Feels'.

The original recording was remixed for the single at Mute's Worldwide Studios with the infamous producer Flood at the mixing desk and Mute boss Daniel Miller overseeing the mastery. We did new vocals and tightened the whole sound up, making it sound more like a radio single.

'This Is How It Feels' was the first single under the new Mute deal, and reached No. 14 in the charts, a massive achievement for a band who, up to that point, had done most of the work themselves, financed by gigging, selling records and T-shirts, and, above all, themselves. I love the fact that thousands of unknown fans bought the record and defended us and our haircuts against detractors in thousands of nightclubs, classrooms, work places and front rooms. I love the fact that, although I didn't write it, that song will follow me to the grave.

*Directing Traffik*
This is a cautionary tale about the dangers of taking too many drugs and frying your brain. The central image is of someone waving a plane into a take-off spot at Manchester airport, or a policeman conducting cars past an accident; an action repeated on a thousand gurning dance floors from Manchester to Moscow, as E-heads weaved their hands uncontrollably round their heads and bodies. At this time, Clint was with Debbie and they were quite anti-drugs, so the song makes an interesting change from the almost ubiquitous drug-fuelled songs of the other contemporary

bands, such as Happy Mondays, The Stone Roses or 808 State, but in one way or another, most of us made up for it later on. The chorus line 'skeleton with skin' apes a line from a Too Much Texas song I wrote back in 1986 called 'Portugal'.

Nick Garside used an early digital compiling machine called an Audiophile to extend some of the pre-verse segments and choruses. The album version of the track is a bit of a mess so when we pieced together a compilation record in 2003, we didn't use this slightly butchered version, favouring an earlier one. It was quite normal for Inspiral Carpets to name different recordings or versions of songs slightly differently to indicate that they were alternatives of the same tracks. An earlier version of the song was spelt 'Directing Traffic', whereas the album track was titled 'Directing Traffik'. A similar fate faced 'Commercial Rain', recorded in 1989, versus the Victor Van Vugt version re-recorded as 'Commercial Reign' in 1990.

*Besides Me*

I wrote the words and a lot of the music for this song, with assistance from Clint and the rest of the band. This was a jolly, upfront pop song, which extolled the virtues of being a young band, taking on the world, and the world coming along with us. I suppose I was recognising that I was in a new gang now, and it was one-for-all and all-for-one! I always think this track sounds like a football song, with its simple, unpretentious, rousing choruses.

*Many Happy Returns*

Graham was an absolute fanatic of the sixties cult television show *The Prisoner*, where Patrick McGoohan played an ex-secret service agent who had been kidnapped and taken to a mysterious village, from which he spent each episode fruitlessly trying to escape. There is an episode called 'Many Happy Returns', which is the seventh of the seventeen episodes, where the nameless prisoner, known only as 'Number 6', escapes the village on a raft, gets back to London and then is tricked by the organisation that kidnapped him in the first place and is taken back to the village. There is no direct reference to the TV show in the song, but titles are usually quite emblematic in Graham's songs.

*Memories Of You*
We were still firmly in the realm of thinking of albums as being vinyl, and thus made up of two sides, when we penned the running order of our first two albums. This song concluded the A-side of the vinyl version of the album and is an experimental, psychedelic instrumental. Clint recorded the vocals of a tramp who used to sit outside Out of the Blue and dropped them onto the end of the song. The tune got its name from the song the tramp was singing; it has a beautiful honesty to it. Clint always loved the idea of including that alienation, making it public – it was the tramp obsession that had been visited previously on the song 'Joe'. It reminds me of 'Jesus Blood Never Failed Me Yet', a piece of orchestral music that composer Gavin Bryars constructed around the loop of a tramp singing.

We would use the segment of music which became 'Memories Of You' as an introduction to the band's live show. It begins quietly, and gradually, as the instruments join the lone Farfisa, it crescendos into an orgy of violent sound. Clint added whale song and a lot of white noise and sounds taken from recordings of tuning in and out of foreign radio stations captured while on holiday. These conflicting kaleidoscopes of sound were added to the projected slides that we included in our shows, like some Andy Warhol/ Factory happening.

## She Comes In The Fall

Graham brought the beginning of the lyrics and the chord structure to 'She Comes In The Fall' into the rehearsal room at Out of the Blue. The title is a bastardisation of a phrase from Roman Polanski's thriller *Rosemary's Baby*, in which the central character is warned of the devil's rebirth in the words 'comes with the fall', which are thrown up as a potential anagram of a book's title, *All of Them Witches*.

The lead and backing vocals have the archetypal question and answer of Clint and myself: Clint's rich Northern vowels with my softer Southern twang. It does have a menacing quality, which comes out in the stampeding rhythm of the drums, and the extended military drum outro. The drums were always a massive part of that indie rock/dance crossover thing that the Haçienda and the whole Manchester vibe was rooted within. Craig drew inspiration from an eclectic pool of records for his drumming for Inspiral Carpets songs; he told us that the drums on this one were influenced by the Kate Bush song 'Cloudbusting'.

Daniel Miller remixed this song for the single release at the in-house studios located on top of Mute's premises. Daniel edited half of the first verse out for the single edit, so that it would get to the chorus sooner. He also added a sample of a demonic guitar, some new vocals by myself, and got us all to add some lively percussion instruments, including vibraslaps, tambourines and God knows what else, to add to the voodoo.

The video for 'She Comes In The Fall' was filmed in the derelict docks and warehouses near London Bridge. The Hornchurch Haverettes provided some visual stimulation in the form of the All Girls Marching Band, twiddling sticks and banging drums to underline the military drumming outro. I wore a heraldic Armand Basi top, patterned with horses and unicorns; it seemed like a good idea at the time.

## Monkey On My Back

This is one of Graham's songs and is an old-style, Steven Holt-era, Inspirals garage-punk extravaganza, with the prerequisite unrequited hate lyrics spat out at top volume over a grinding backing. Love is described here as an addictive drug.

## Sun Don't Shine

A melodic, romantic song, which makes it stand out on this album. It's another song that goes back to the original line-up of the band. We tried to play it live, but I found the key too low for my tenor voice. It isn't anything like it, but there is something in the spirit of the song that reminds me of Duran Duran's 'Save a Prayer'.

## Inside My Head

Two minutes of garage-punk explosion. It is the kind of classic early Inspirals song which musically pitches the band somewhere between the psychedelic West Coast US bands of the sixties – like the Seeds, 13th Floor Elevators, The Chocolate Watchband – and seventies punk bands like the Stranglers.

## Move

Graham said wryly that this song was about a man fingering his girlfriend while she was asleep. This I take as being a piece of humorous obscurification. I sang a held-note at the end of the song, which I thought was the sort of touch that Morrissey might have added to a Smiths' single. I have always loved singles where there is a little guitar solo that kicks in on the fade-out, which makes you want to put the whole song back on again.

While we were recording 'Move', John Robb was ploughing the furrow that Inspiral Carpets were little more than Stone Roses copyists. When I met John socially he asked me what the band were up to. I wickedly replied, 'Just trying to sound more like The Stone Roses.'

*Sackville*

The closing track on the album is a heart-rending song written by Clint. Sackville Street was a red-light district which adjoined the Gay Village. You could watch the prostitutes and rent boys at work outside, bombed out of their heads. At this time I was living in the warehouse on Sackville Street, where Alison ran her clothes business. This was the same building that Kevin Cummins shot his iconic Stone Roses *NME* cover, where they were all covered in paint. On one occasion, a pipe burst within the warehouse and all the paint from the long-ago photo shoot pissed down the walls, leaving my old bike covered in a set of streaky, Jackson Pollock-style Pop Art colours.

The room above ours was used as a studio by Matt and Pat, or Central Station as they were known, who did the album artwork for Happy Mondays and Northside, amongst others. Johnson/Panas, the graphic designers who created all the Haçienda posters and tickets, were up there too.

Clint would drive from Oldham to Manchester with his air-driven pump organ* to teach me Inspiral Carpets songs. Clint must have found Sackville Street to be a culture shock after what he was used to, and he wrote a song about what he saw out of our gaff's windows. This song captures that moment perfectly, my bohemian lifestyle informing Clint's writing to a quite beautiful end.

*Life* was released on 23rd April 1990 and got to No. 2 in the UK charts. An extended version was later released in the US. When I listen to it now, I hear a raw, garagey, DIY record.

*This is the very organ launched unceremoniously into a lake on the moors in the promotional video for 'This Is How It Feels'.

# 7

## The 8:15 from Manchester

Binsey was asked if we could supply the theme tune to a new Saturday-morning kids' show called *The 8:15 from Manchester* that was to go on air over the summer, while the stalwart *Going Live* took a break. We were duly invited to the BBC to discuss a project that could be mutually beneficial. We would get a weekly blast of our tune to a potentially massive audience, whilst they would look modern and Northern and 'cool' in their branding. Our idea was to supply an instrumental version of an old Steven Holt-era song called 'Head For The Sun', with its psychedelic 'ba ba ba ba's and positive pumping sixties vibe. We recorded a rough version in Out of the Blue, but the TV production team were having none of it, they wanted us instead to re-record our third single 'Find Out Why', so we stuck the 'ba ba ba ba's on that instead. The first of a series of disappointments was the fee: doing the theme tune attracted a measly £250 waiver on performance rights. Never look a gift horse in the mouth! But it was good, and instant exposure.

We let them film us recording the theme in their rather poorly equipped audio studios, and they filmed a whole strand for the first show where we shared the spotlight with a new teen band called Take That making an early TV appearance. I remember Robbie saying that the band loved The Stone Roses, Happy Mondays and Inspiral Carpets. Strategically he had just bagged all our young fans and annexed them to their star-strung career wagon train.

One idea that never got developed was for the show to create a comedy strand where Inspiral Carpets would have a little cartoon section, in which they would make up little narratives for us, a kind of proto Monkees. We eschewed the project. If we had pursued this to its fullest reaches – who knows where it might have gone? Years later, after much pot boiling, this idea became realised as S Club 7.

In 1990 we booked into Konk Studios in Hornsey, in order to re-record the song 'Commercial Rain', at Daniel Miller's request. He wanted it to be released as a single in the United States, and to be included in an expanded version of *Life*. Konk Studios was owned by Ray Davies of the Kinks; Gold records covered the walls of the office upstairs. The studio boasted the very desk that Pink Floyd recorded *The Dark Side of the Moon* on at Abbey Road, which had been accidentally set on fire at some time in the seventies, then rebuilt and automated to make mixes easier. They also had a non-functioning Mellotron, the beautiful tape-based pre-synthesiser keyboard which The Beatles used on the intro to 'Strawberry Fields Forever'.

The Kinks were recording a song in the other studio while we were there in 1990. A year and a half later, when we popped back in to do some extra vocal overdubs on a song from our third album, The Kinks were still struggling with the same song. One day, Ray Davies arrived in the studio with a couple of black eyes and a split lip. Ray and his brother Dave were notorious for fighting. Clint, ever the diplomat, immediately questioned the veteran singer about how he had got injured. Ray, embarrassed, answered that he had walked into a sink. Clint put his hand in the air in guestimation, and asked if the sink was roughly Dave Davies' height.

Our daily jaunt from our rented apartments in Muswell Hill to the studio in Hornsey would always be broken with a stop-off outside 23 Cranley Gardens, the last home of the 'Muswell Hill Murderer' Dennis Nilsen. The stop-off was made to satisfy Graham's obsession with serial killers and have a 'murder tourist' peek around. Nilsen befriended his kills, either by picking them up in gay bars or in his capacity of working with the homeless. He killed fifteen men and boys, dismembered their bodies and put them down the drain. A neighbour, complaining about blocked drains, called Dyno-Rod to clear them. Nilsen forlornly poured the contents of a KFC bargain bucket down the drain as a decoy, but was rumbled once the hapless drain engineer began to find human thigh bones amongst the fried chicken.

# 8

## Throw your caution into the wind

In 1990 we completed our first American tour. The Gulf War was happening and consequently the transatlantic and domestic air flights were entirely empty – Americans were just too jumpy and worried about terrorism to fly. It was eerie to sit in the bowels of a 747 with no one but ourselves and the stewardesses, who instantly upgraded us to first class and plied us with endless drinks, while I chain-smoked the journey away, or took a kip on the floor at the back near the toilets.

We flew into Washington DC and I wondered if the Promised Land actually looked like it did on the television programmes like *Batman*, *The Waltons* or *Starsky and Hutch*. As we stepped off the plane, Oleta Adams' song 'Get Here' was playing on the concourse bus. 'You can reach me on an airplane, you can reach me with your mind.' It underlined the sheer distance that we had travelled, both in miles and experience.

The first night we went out and watched a solo concert by Lloyd Cole. The following day we played at the 9:30 Club, a dingy basement of an old theatre in exactly the part of town where Abraham Lincoln was assassinated. After the show, the bar staff were glassing rats that lived in the bottle skips outside. Mark Coyle, our monitor engineer, and Noel asked the promoter where they could get some 'bush' (meaning grass). He thought they meant prostitutes and recommended some brothels. Once they had corrected this cultural misunderstanding, he suggested they went to a black neighbourhood, where they found a man who took $20 from them and said he would be back in a minute with the grass. He opened up and walked through the door of a big old city townhouse. After five minutes the guy hadn't come back, so Noel and Mark banged on the door. When it went unanswered they tentatively opened it, and stepped through to find that the whole row of houses was knocked through and held up by scaffolding on the other side of the door. The man and their money was long gone.

We weren't just touring in the US, we were also working hand-in-hand with Mute as bait to negotiate a new US label deal for their entire artist roster. There was a scramble from all eleven major US labels wanting to ingratiate themselves with us. This charge began in London over the summer of 1990 when Michael Rosenblatt, son of WEA distribution honcho Ed Rosenblatt, took us to a Soho restaurant called Topo Gigio; named after an Italian cartoon mouse. A John Cleese-like waiter kept on asking us if we wanted more 'miserable water', presumably a London-Italian alternative to mineral water. We got Michael drunk and then dumped him in the middle of a busy dual carriageway at midnight, shouting abuse at him, which of course he loved every minute of. American record company execs are so used to being arse-licked back in America that they enjoyed this eccentric treatment.

The American major record company rout culminated with a black comedy moment: us sitting in the offices of Geffen Records on Sunset Strip in Los Angeles with David Geffen. We'd arrived into LA with Eazy-E's 'It Takes Two' playing as we rode the highway into the metropolis; the 'whoa's and 'yeah's of the track exploding into our excitement. Geffen was meeting Oldham's finest in a pretentious Starship Enterprise of a record company office, and this $4.6 billionaire was witnessing Craig removing his sweaty trainers and picking his feet (comparatively mild bodily behaviour for him) while Graham grilled him in relation to which bands his label had dropped recently. Graham asked David Geffen what he thought of our music. He responded with, 'I haven't heard your music. I pay people to do that for me.'

In the mid-eighties my brother Andrew had been briefly signed to Geffen Records as part of a band called Mummy Calls. The band's debut album had cost some $250,000 to record. I organised a bunch of student friends to buy their single 'Beauty Has Her Way' at a selection of record shops over the North West of England to try to help nudge it into the lower reaches of the charts, but to no avail. Partly because of this family circumstance, I was wary of Geffen Records; a major American conglomerate, it was no Mute Records for sure.

Ken Friedman, who in 1990 worked as an A&R man for A&M, met us on the tour. He had the indignity of having managed The Smiths when they split up in America in 1987. Some fans blame him personally for the deterioration of Johnny Marr and Morrissey's relationship, and the band's demise at that time. I was schmoozed by Ken at the end of a drunken night. I teased him by saying that if he signed fellow Manchester band Northside to A&M, he could forget about ever signing Inspirals. My teasing statement was sprung at the very end of the night, in perfect timing as the lift doors snapped in front of his face, allowing no reply on his behalf, and I ascended to my hotel room and certainty.

We eventually signed to Elektra, along with the rest of the Mute catalogue.

While in LA, Terry Christian interviewed us for the first ever edition of the controversial TV show *The Word*. Terry was a local DJ from Piccadilly Radio and a supporter of

Inspiral Carpets. *The Word* got its name from the indie pop page of the *Manchester Evening News*, which was published every Friday, and Terry wrote for it. He was ensconced in LA, drinking heavily and proving very popular. The filming process was a bit of a struggle, with a cameraman and director filming us walking down Sunset Strip, asking us to go into a tattoo parlour, then insisting that we walk down the strip again because the previous shot wasn't good enough. Eventually we got a bit pissed off because they didn't seem to know what they were doing and we wanted to explore LA in between meeting David Geffen and the gig.

Before we left LA we went to the legendary rock station KROQ and met Rodney Bingenheimer, the famous Ramones hair-styled DJ who has seen all comers in the music scene since the early sixties and had introduced glam rock to the states. KROQ had as many listeners as Radio 1 had in the UK. This was massive for a little band from England.

In San Francisco we played the Whisky A Go Go in the Haight-Ashbury area, which was awash with old junkies and stoners and tramps. Some old fakers tried to sell us 'tar' outside the venue, the local name for smack. After the show, Clint, Graham and Martyn met some nurses who took them to see the house where the Grateful Dead had lived in the sixties with all their Deadhead graffiti on the walls now painted over with white acrylic paint. We saw an old Farfisa keyboard in a music shop that we hoped had previously belonged to Ray Manzarek of The Doors. While visiting Elektra, we met the engineer Bruce Botnick, who recorded The Doors' albums, working with Paul A. Rothchild.

In New York, we played at the Limelight Club, where the English ex-pat promoters Tony Fletcher and Neville Wells booked us. Huey from Fun Lovin' Criminals worked as a cocktail waiter in the bar upstairs. Dave Gahan from

Depeche Mode came backstage after our show like some rock Frankie Howard; he was so pissed that he fell over and banged his head on a table. Clint responded to this by saying 'Come on, David, behave yourself – you aren't in Basildon now, you know.' Dave later shagged a girl in the dressing room toilet cubicle.

Daniel Miller took us to a Cajun restaurant which was hidden from the New York streets behind a fence of wooden boards covered in graffiti. Once in the place, there were luxuriant lush green plants and palms and beautiful French-speaking waitresses. The food was first class and the vibe *Angel Heart*. We drove out of New York through a large industrial hinterland, where our driver told us that local life expectancy was low due to the large quantity of chemicals that induced cancers in the local population.

Our first trip to America had been everything we had hoped for, and had surpassed all expectations.

# 9

## It's a different world

We arrived at Narita airport, dazed from an eight-hour flight with Japan Airlines, during which we were given paper slippers to wear. We were greeted by a Beatles-esque mobbing at the arrivals hall and the flashing of professional and amateur cameras. Our charges from the Japanese promotion and record companies gave us the traditional business gifts of bottles of sake containing floating flakes of gold, and digital wristwatches with the name of the promotions company written on them. We were driven to the Tokyo Prince Hotel, the same one where, twenty years earlier, my eldest brother had married his Japanese bride, Masako Tomonaga, against the wishes of her family.

The photographer Kevin Cummins had been commissioned by *Vox* magazine to record a photo journalistic piece. In typical Mute style, the international department of the UK record label had somehow half agreed to pay for a room for Kevin to stay in the hotel, but had failed to follow it through, resulting in him being temporarily homeless. Clint generously offered up his hotel room and bunked up with Graham, a characteristically thoughtful, practical and kind response.

Outside the hotel was a small park with a Shinto shrine in it. A stand-off began, as a raggle-taggle of Japanese Inspirals fans beseeched us and tried to get into the hotel and up to our bedrooms. The hotel security intervened when any of them smuggled their way in. Clint's reaction to jet lag and the cultural alienation was to wake up in the middle of the night, go out into the hotel corridor and shriek a blood-curdling, full-volume existential scream, which was incredibly funny.

We had a record company executive called Nobbi, who worked for Mute's Japanese licensee, Alfa Records. Nobbi was an obsessive Mute devotee; his boss eventually sacked him because he absented himself from his desk for a week whilst walking round Tokyo dressed up as an Inspiral Carpets cow. Riding on the Tokyo underground with all the Inspirals, Clint leant forward and tried to remove – in one swift decisive hand movement – a loose hair that appeared to have landed on Nobbi's face. Unfortunately, a small lump of skin lifted with the hair as it pinged out. The hair was attached to a mole, and a noticeable piece of blood and flesh exited with it as Nobbi shrieked. The reaction in the crowded train carriage was electric; everyone else was Japanese, and what they saw was a European invading a Japanese man's personal space and assaulting him. Added to the mix was the fact that facial hairs in moles are seen as being lucky and a sign of long life and virility in Japanese culture. It was like a scene from an as yet unmade David Lynch film mixing horror, fear and loathing and humour in a heady broth. We went to a nightclub filled predominantly with middle-aged businessmen and I nearly got beaten up for stupidly putting my feet on a table. I quickly learnt that feet, in Japanese culture, are considered to be very dirty.

Nobbi took us to the oldest restaurant in Tokyo. We nearly didn't make it because some of the band and crew became impatient as we waited for an hour in the hotel foyer for the record company big-wigs to show up. Eventually the execs arrived and we decamped to the restaurant where they cooked the best food I had ever eaten, a seemingly never-ending thirty-course meal. We were sat around a large table with individual cooks assigned to each of us, and they cut up raw meat and vegetables, theatrically spilling the unwanted bits down the front of their aprons, where they would then fall down into a recess under the table. The chefs would juggle the ingredients into a wok, and then pass the cooked dish to diners, using a long paddle to cover the ten-foot distance between us and them.

One well-documented difficulty in Anglo-Japanese relations is deference. This meant that when we were asking Japanese record company or business managers a question, and they wanted to reply in the negative, they would use the Japanese word for 'yes' but with an inflection which, to the trained and experienced ear, is a millionth less enthusiastic than if it was said to actually mean 'YES!' Deference, conformity and a strict sense of where one fits into the hierarchy and natural order of things are the reasons that there is some truth in the clichéd narrative of middle-aged Japanese businessmen who have lost their jobs visiting the park each day with their briefcase, for years on end, to avoid the embarrassment of telling their wives and children that no, they don't have a job any longer. This is also why the kids love the anarchy, spontaneity and classlessness suggested by rock and roll, psychedelia and pop. One misconception about the Japanese is that they take themselves very seriously, and nothing could be further from the truth.

Japan was amazing. We enjoyed the Beatles-esque mobbing of the fans, the concerts where the audience would sit and clap dutifully, the electronics shops where we bought consumer durables and saw the future of hard-disc recording and personal stereos.

Each of the industries that helped Japan emerge from post-war surrender in the forties has its own iconic totem: the Tokyo Tower is the one for the steel and construction industries. I went up it and was amused by the fact that this testament to the power of human spirit and recovery built on such a massive scale was painted exactly the same shade of orange as Salford Van Hire vehicles.

# 10

## I'm going to build a monument

A curious triangulation exerted itself over the 'Big Three' bands who rose to fame in what became known as the 'Madchester' scene. The Stone Roses were the first out of the block, their local fame exploding in 1989 onto the national psyche with the release of their eponymous debut record. As their star was ascendant, Happy Mondays were then thrust onto the national consciousness crooning 'Hallelujah' on *Top of the Pops* with Kirsty MacColl in November 1989. Then Inspiral Carpets arrived in a big way in March 1990. I always felt that each of the three bands were always looking over their shoulders feverishly, feeling a mixture of camaraderie and scorn for the band that followed them. For The Stone Roses it was Happy Mondays, for Happy Mondays it was us, and for us it was The Charlatans.

My first chance to see Happy Mondays up close was in June 1989, when Inspiral Carpets did the Valencia Rock Festival *La Conjura de las Danzas* for the Spanish John Peel, Jorge Albi. We flew out to Spain along with Happy Mondays, a Brighton band called The Pop Guns and The La's.

Lee Mavers and John Power from The La's played 'Timeless Melody' acoustically to a few of us on a stone balcony above the club before they took to the stage and blew everyone else away. It was the best thing I had ever heard. Lee had a blocked nose and a sore throat and I asked him if he used Olbas Oil to clear it – he went mad with me and said that it would eat away at the knares of his nose. I found this advice a bit rich, considering some of the materials that he had allegedly put up his nose and into his body over the years.

We'd flown Clint's Farfisa Compact Duo over to the gig, but neglected to take a guitar. The crappy, cheap semi-acoustic guitar Graham borrowed wouldn't get or stay in tune, so after a horribly out-of-tune 'Joe', he mimed his way through the gig, and we learned to take our own guitars to the next overseas show.

Shaun Ryder had fallen asleep for hours on the beach, stoned, before waking up very sunburnt and as pink as Salford salmon. Clint asked if he had checked out any girls on the beach, and Shaun told him that he was in too much pain to pay any attention. Happy Mondays finally took to the stage at 7 o'clock in the morning and played their way through a typically shambolic, bad-tempered but classic performance with Shaun suffering, while dolly girls swung overhead on gigantic circus-style swings hanging from the roof of the club.

A few London-based journalists from *Sounds* magazine, including David Cavanagh, had left their cameras, credit cards and possessions in the communal dormitory where we all slept. Happy Mondays had travelled with an entourage and when all the bands, journalists and photographers were transported back to the hotel a lot of shouting transpired. The poor hapless hotelier burst into the room to give us a bollocking and, like children, we all pretended to be asleep. It was only once the hotelier had left that the journalists realised that all their stuff had been stolen, presumably by some of the Mondays' 'mates'. Of course, we didn't leave anything there in the first place.

In November 1989, Alison and I went to see Happy Mondays play at the Free Trade Hall. We didn't have tickets, but Alison and her friend, Jane Roberts, knew the Mondays' manager, Nathan McGough. Nathan was the son of Mersey

Poet and The Scaffold member, Roger McGough. We weren't on the guest list, but we approached the stage door and luckily Nathan saw us and dragged us in, along with what must have been over half of the audience.

When the Mondays came on stage, there was so much ganja smoke in the hall, mixed with dry ice, that you couldn't see any of the band – all you could see were vague shapes, eclipsed from behind by the frequent visual stab of the lights of sequencers. It looked like the end of *ET*, when the aliens stand on the prow of the spaceship, blemished by a flood of light. It was the best concert I have ever seen.

John Robb, who was the singer with the Blackpool punk band The Membranes and aspiring journalist, interviewed Clint in 1989 about the emergent Happy Mondays. What Clint said about the band was that they were very impressive and played in a way where being technically good wasn't as important as the mood and vibe that they created with their music. Some sub-editor altered the quote to infer that Clint had said that Happy Mondays couldn't play their instruments, a typical strategy in the press to deliberately misquote someone in order to start a print war of words.

Of course Happy Mondays then started slagging Inspiral Carpets off through the press. Shaun Ryder's attack on us culminated in a *Face* interview where he branded us collectively as 'clueless knobheads' while Bez said that we all pretended that we took Ecstasy when we didn't. Shaun also made a comment that we were bread-heads, motivated by money, and said that the idea of making a living from playing music made him feel sick.

The general heat between the Inspirals and the Mondays was elevated further when Noel was working in the Cow office and filled in a questionnaire for *Record Mirror* in Clint's name. Noel answered the question 'What is your favourite Happy Mondays track?' with the controversial answer 'God's

Cop (smackhead remix)' and faxed it back to *Record Mirror*, who subsequently printed it. Word was going round that Shaun wasn't pleased about this and was on the warpath seeking out Clint to beat him up.

I decided to go and see the Mondays play at Wembley Arena in the summer of 1990 at the height of our war of words. Alison and I stayed at the Swiss Cottage Holiday Inn (near London Zoo) which must have been considered quite a plush hotel when it was first built back in the seventies, as it made quite a few appearances in episodes of *The Sweeney*, with plastic TV gangsters, played by people like Patrick Mower swimming in the hotel pool while verbally getting it from Regan and Carter. In the lift on the way up to the room, I met Mark Day, the Mondays' guitarist. He was surprised to see me there, and asked why we were staying in the hotel. I explained that we were coming to see them play that night.

The gig was great, and I met an American A&R man from Elektra called Jon Leshay. The Mondays and Inspirals were both signed to Elektra in the States, so it was good to meet him. I was wearing a £2000 Thierry Mugler leather jacket that had metal tusks for buttons – Jon really liked it, and we agreed that if he helped Inspirals sell a million records, he could have it in return.

After the show, I went backstage and approached Shaun Ryder. I got talking to him and said that I enjoyed the show and that I had heard that he wasn't pleased with Clint for the comments he was supposed to have made about Happy Mondays. I told him that someone else had filled in the questionnaire and that it wasn't Clint. I didn't say that it was Noel because I didn't want to drop him in it. Shaun said he didn't believe me, so I said that we should go outside to sort it out. At this point he backed down and became as nice as pie, which was pretty much the last time that Shaun publicly slagged our band off. So that was that, although you wont find this anecdote in his autobiography!

In the summer of 1989, when Inspirals were exploding all over the place, we got wind of the fact that Brian Turner had put the word out that Happy Mondays were planning to do a headline show at the 12,000-capacity GMEX centre. Apparently Inspiral Carpets would be supporting them. This was news to us.

GMEX was the old central station – closed in the late sixties – that lay empty for twenty years until the Development Corporation spent £20 million putting a new glass roof on it. The Factory Manchester music extravaganza Festival of the Tenth Summer had been held there in July 1986, you can see this event immortalised in a picture of the audience set against the outline of the arched roof in the centre gatefold of the vinyl version of The Smiths' album, *Rank*.

The Mondays' audacious plan was something that we weren't keen to be part of. We could see the trajectory that both bands were on, and we didn't want to be labelled as Happy Mondays' pet support band, to be judged and characterised by their eccentric and hilarious actions (although we did love their music and attitude). Sat in our Sackville Street office, Binsey had the phone in his hand and told Brian Turner that we weren't up for the support. When Brian asked why, Binsey cupped his hands over the phone's receiver and stage whispered, 'Why don't you want to do it?' We all looked at one another until I replied, 'Because we are going to do our own headline show at the GMEX.' Everyone swallowed, and Binsey gave Brian the rather surprising answer.

Later that day we contacted Simon Moran, who at that time was a relatively small regional indie promoter. We put the idea of a headline GMEX show to him. He said that he would promote a show at GMEX on one proviso, that we would underwrite the £23,000 hire fee for the show in case the whole thing went wrong.

The concert was legendary and immortalised through its video release *21.7.90*, which demonstrates how big the band were at that time. We threw in all the trimmings – a fantastic light show and drum majorettes from The Hornchurch Haverettes to introduce 'She Comes In The Fall'. Support was supplied by The La's and the Hull-based band Ashley and Jackson.

John Craven's daughter, Vicky, was an Inspirals fan. She followed us around during 1990 to various shows, and she was at the GMEX gig, sitting with her dad in the VIP seats next to Tim Booth of James and the rest of his band mates. It goes without saying that you probably shouldn't touch any open drinks that may be left in a dressing room when you come backstage. That night Craig dipped his cock in one of four glasses of mineral water which were left on the table. When Vicky and John Craven came backstage, Craig mischievously offered the ex-*Multi-Coloured Swap Shop* presenter a drink. Of course I remember in slow motion now how he stumbled towards the first prize of the unsuspecting 'cocktail', a moment of surrealism heightened at that particular second as two of my school friends from Abingdon walked in. I introduced them to a now-quenched John Craven, but they thought I was being funny until they did a double-take and realised that it was the TV star from our youth. I still can't count the many levels of irony that were captured in that one scene.

Pete Walsh snapped the band out the back of the building, underneath a large letter 'E' which was painted on the outside of the exhibition centre – a cheeky and rather clichéd jokey reference to Ecstasy. I sat behind the wheel of a Mercedes 380SL sports car which someone had left parked there. Pete photographed me as I snorted, 'I'd never buy a car like this'. A week later, I was the owner of a silver second-hand Mercedes 380SL. Alison had bought it without me, while I was down in London. Mute weren't happy at all. Mick Patterson, the in-house press officer, who must've been having a hard time promoting me as a typical, working-class, Northern chap, wasn't pleased by the nouveau riche *loadsamoney* connotations of the picture and the purchase. Naturally, the band didn't allow me to live down what I had said about never buying such a car, and they carried out a genuinely hilarious wind-up some months later. They got hold of a repair invoice for the car, and Graham used his printing skills and a fax machine to forge a letter from Interpol claiming that the car had been involved in a car-ringing scandal. After bollocking my wife for buying a stolen car, I called the French phone number from the Cow office phone. The French office of Mute answered, and I knew that, once again, I had been had, good and proper.

GMEX is one of the two occasions where I have been reminded by fans, long after the event, of an act of kindness that I had carried out. Apparently there were quite a few fans standing at the back of the venue begging for tickets, so I went back inside and got six tickets for a group who were really grateful. It's good to hear positive stories relating to this time of my life, to know that I was capable of kindness and wasn't always a total wanker, even if the effects of fame were mostly negative, and examples of good behaviour few and far between.

# 11

## We all pray for simple things

I attended a concert by The Charlatans at the Royal Court in Liverpool. The venue was a lovely Victorian theatre, and I remember traipsing through the section underneath the stage to go and give my congratulations to the band for an impressive and well received performance. Before I got to the dressing room, I spied a young girl sprawled on the floor in agony from a broken or severely twisted ankle. There was a St John Ambulance person attending to her as she screamed out. As I walked past, her face lit up in recognition and she temporarily forgot about her ankle as I lent down to give her a kiss. I was at the height of my fame and its power worked like clinical heroin on her pain, like some kind of Indie Jesus. If only for just a few seconds.

Sometime in 1990 I was out in Didsbury with Alison, her friend Jane Roberts and Jane's boyfriend, Peter Hook. Peter had witnessed the stellar rise of the whole Manchester movement, and seen how Inspirals had been dragged through from popular indie also-rans into one of the nation's biggest three bands in a matter of months in 1989. Hooky said something to me that morning that initially annoyed me – he said that the fame we had found wasn't real, that it would wane and we should be ready for that eventuality. I didn't react well to this advice, and thought at the time he was being obtuse. In retrospect it was one of the most caring and accurate pieces of advice I have been given.

On 25th August 1990 Inspiral Carpets headlined the Saturday night of the Reading Festival. The bill that day included The Wedding Present, The Buzzcocks and Billy Bragg. We arrived at the festival the day before and booked into the local hotel with an enormous entourage of forty people. I rode round Reading city centre with members of the band Candy Flip in the infamous Mercedes with the soft top. On the Friday night we watched the headline set from The Pixies. We chatted to them in the hotel afterwards and were blown away by how down to earth they were, versus how wonderful, powerful and sentient they were on stage.

On the afternoon of the gig I booked a music industry car to pick my parents up from Oxford and drive them to the festival. My mother and father had never seen me perform, except as Macheath in *The Threepenny Opera* at Larkmead School, whereupon my father thought I was rubbish. Of course, they had absolutely no concept of the scale of the festival. When they arrived, Simon from the Mean Fiddler installed them safely on the side of the stage and John Peel bought them both a Guinness. What a privilege to have the two most significant alpha males in my life meeting in one place and time.

The concert was amazing as we rocked 80,000 revellers. We decided to start the show by releasing £6000 worth of fireworks, the idea being that it wasn't the obvious option, and that it might get more of the crowd to come out of their tents and watch us. Unfortunately the hood over the stage prevented us from witnessing even ten pence worth of fireworks, although John Peel captured them on Super 8 and we watched them some time later. We started the performance with the two female dancers from Ashley and Jackson dancing in a pantomime cow outfit. Rumours continue to this day that it was Noel in the cow, but it wasn't.

After the gig, seeking parental support, I asked my father what he thought of the show. He said, 'The last time I saw an audience react like that was when I saw Mussolini give a speech in Rome in 1939.' Praise indeed!

## XII

### The Black Light

# III
## *The Beast Inside*

# 12

## I steal to feed

1991 saw the shattering of the remainders of the Manchester movement. A friend, Jane, had been drinking in the tacky bar within Sacha's Hotel and was dragged up to the dance floor by some leather-jacketed punky metal head. They had traipsed around the dance floor, piss-taking the suited office workers and their tragic molls, aping their shit dance moves, until a tall, aggressive blonde dragged the man away from Jane and the dance floor. This was Kurt Cobain and Courtney Love, who were staying at the hotel. It must have been like meeting Jesus Christ at Blockbusters, or Chairman Mao at the launderette! Clint witnessed Nirvana mesmerise a Reading Festival audience that year. A few saw the Seattle band play in Manchester itself.

Courtney Love was a hangover from the eighties Liverpool scene where she used to hang out with Pete de Freitas from Echo & the Bunnymen. My friend Jem Kelly of The Wild Swans and The Lotus Eaters taught Courtney her first fleeting guitar chords back in the early eighties.

So, Nirvana and the coming wave of grunge was one of the waves of fashion that were breaking over the shoreline and washing away the Madchester sandcastle. Another sign came in the form of a review in *Melody Maker* in the spring of 1991. The editor Steve Sutherland was waxing lyrical about a new band he was tipping as the next big thing. He almost sounded like a lover, describing them with the proud banner: 'Suede, the best new band in Britain'. They hadn't even released a single.

# 13

## I read it in a book in school

Prior to setting off for our first trip to Japan, the rest of the band had tricked me into believing that our tour manager Andrew Mansi had a bad back and couldn't travel with us. The joke was probably based on the fact that the rest of the band and management couldn't deal with my neurotic concerns and sticking my nose in things that weren't strictly my business. Later, when we were recording in Horsham, in the middle of a wind-up session Craig admitted that the story about Mansi's back was a joke. I exploded in annoyance and Craig hit me. The cap I was wearing flew off my head and I cried out in frustrated tears: 'He hit me!' Once again, members of the band seemed to be trying to make my life unbearable.

Steve Rouson, a rockabilly-quiffed keep-fit freak who used to drive for us, took me aside afterwards and said, supportively, that I had to remember that the rest of the band still lived at home, were quite young, and they could do with growing up a bit. I put the situation into context and it made it easier to bear the mimicking taunts of 'He hit me', which still continue to this day.

Mansi came to us through our record label, Mute. He had previously worked for Depeche Mode, both in their office and on the road. He's London-Italian, and has prominent front teeth, which earned him the nickname 'Beaver' or 'Beeve' from the band. He's an Arsenal fan and always full of amusing stories and retorts. Some of the strategies that Mansi would use to get problems solved were both entertaining and educational. In 1994 we played a festival in Tuscany. We were flying straight out afterwards to play at Glastonbury, but the van got stuck in a traffic jam on a mountain road and, after a nail-biting two hours, we eventually got to the airport, just as the plane was about to leave for London. Mansi somehow got us on the plane – I think he may have told airport staff that we were Depeche Mode or Paul McCartney. Any old shit just as long as we got on the plane. Impressive stuff.

Mansi would turn up in a Latin country and start quizzing the promoter about the details of our return transport back to the airport. If they were vague or unhelpful, he would say, 'Look, I am Italian and I know how badly stuff can be organised by you lot, so I want the bus here three hours before the flight.' If we were being ignored at hotel check-ins, he had a signal which would summon us to the front desk where we would start being slightly rude and swearing a bit in front of other guests. It's amazing how quickly we would get service after that.

Mansi's finest hour, however, was when we were doing a non-stop thirty-two-hour trip on a sleeper bus from Minneapolis to Los Angeles. The bus was from the Florida Bus Company, and it was beautiful, with a massive stencil of a surfer emblazoned along the side. A southerner called John Schott drove the bus. John was a redneck, and he would sit in the cab listening to one of a hundred country radio stations. He would flick through a well-thumbed address book and work out which of the several women contained within he knew in the particular state/city we were stopping at. He called these women his 'future ex-wives'.

John was at the depot of the Florida Bus Company on the fateful day that Randy Rhoads, Ozzy Osborne's guitarist, went up in a small plane and flew over the drivers at the depot, before apparently grabbing hold of the plane's controls and crashing to the ground, and his death, in front of them all.

Our bus had a lot of memorabilia from bands who had used it extensively before. The walls had a couple of guitars from The Smithereens fixed on them, and John Schott was naturally proud of his bus and wanted to keep it nice. However, the Happy Mondays had also used the same bus, and there was a story that Shaun Ryder would piss out of the side of his bunk onto the floor, and that during a drunken session the band had broken a cupboard on the bus. When John found out about these acts he was outraged, because it was his home, his bus and his life. He produced a shotgun and requested $500 for the repair. This settled the dispute. Inspirals were therefore well warned not to damage the bus in any way, as we really liked John, and we really didn't want to be staring down the barrel of a redneck's shotgun.

The long drive between Minneapolis and Los Angeles was of course too long for John to do on his own in one go, so Clint took over for five hours while John sparked out, dead to the world, on the long seat behind the driver's cab. There were seven-foot snowdrifts outside, and the door was frozen in a way that prevented it from closing. The band and Mansi were drinking margaritas made using ice taken from the snowdrifts and spun round in a fifties-style electric food mixer. Eventually, Mansi got uncontrollably drunk and lost it. He went mad and ripped one of The Smithereens' guitars off the wall. Craig, who was (at that time) easily the least responsible member of the band, when thrust into a moment of responsibility ran up to Clint in the driver's seat and said that he must stop the bus immediately, because the tour manager had gone mad. Clint explained that he didn't actually know how to stop the bus because he had just jumped into the seat when John jumped out of it – he only knew how to accelerate and change the gears. John slept on through the mayhem like a corpse.

Graham managed to wrestle Mansi back to his bunk, where he sat on him until he agreed not to continue trashing the bus, but as soon as Graham released his grip, Mansi was once again up like a shot and he ripped the other guitar off the wall. At this point, Graham, mindful of the shotgun treatment that might be awaiting us on John's awakening, extracted a confession from him and recorded it on a Walkman. Mansi tried to break free once more, but Graham booted him in the face, and that was the end of the wilful pissed-up Mansi.

The next day, Mansi was fifty percent hungover and fifty percent embarrassed by his rock and roll vandalism. John thought it was funny and accepted some money for the damages. We drove on for another sixteen hours until we reached Los Angeles.

# 14

## Don't count your chicken
## before he crawls out of his shell

In between our first and second albums we recorded the *Island Head* EP. The EP was recorded by Gareth Jones, but because Chris Nagle had been brought in to 'save the mixes', he was duly appointed producer for our new album. We began the process of amassing the material for the album by individually bringing songs in to the rehearsal room and then communally sewing and welding them into a collective Inspiral whole. We moved rehearsal rooms from Bloom Street to a place in Denton. The plan was to get Chris to visit us at the rehearsal room in order to make basic recordings of the songs and suggestions on arrangements. Once this process of preproduction was complete, we could then decamp to a residential studio in Horsham called Ridge Farm to do the recording, before mixing the songs at Strawberry Studios in Stockport.

We had an in-house cook at Ridge Farm called Laura. As employers, Inspiral Carpets were incapable of keeping a professional separation between workers and friends. When we arrived Laura was very pleasant and everyone got on fine, but after Graham made a couple of jokes about her chest size, the barriers were down and within just two days she was serving up the food with a fag in her hand. Sometime later, Laura appeared on *The Word*, where she took part in a wet T-shirt contest – so her attributes must have been legendary in the early nineties music scene, and we clearly weren't the only ones to spot them!

Lyrically *The Beast Inside* was to be darker than the garage pop of our debut album; it was a high watermark in terms of Clint's enthusiasm for songwriting. Rather than record a simple follow-up to the garagey *Life*, we decided to strike out for an album that mixed the less obvious. While we were on tour in Europe, we had taken a trip to Dachau and witnessed the site of Nazi atrocities, and one idea was to call the record *Never Again* after the sculpture that stands on the site of the concentration camp. The inside sleeve of the vinyl record contains a pattern which is influenced by the barbed-wire-like sculpture.

We included ten songs on the finished album:

*Caravan*
With its snaking arabesque keyboard lines, vocal harmonies and Balearic house-style piano, this song is every bit a pop record. David Keane of Oldham band Asia Fields added percussion in the form of congas. The words of the song came from Graham, and are about the Nazi Death marches that concentration camp inmates were put through in the dying days of the war. I added the line: 'Live for every day as if it were the last.' This spirit of *carpe diem* being thrown in to show any critics that we were perfectly aware that we were enjoying our time in the sun.

*Please Be Cruel*
I wrote the words and music, which were subtly welded into an Inspirals song by the rest of the entourage. The title is a wordplay on Elvis' 'Don't Be Cruel' and is a small masochistic nod to the song's subject matter. It fits in perfectly with the darker themes and mood of the second album. Based around a little sixties-styled descending scale of a guitar riff, in the way that The Stone Roses' 'Waterfall',

or The Beatles' 'Dear Prudence' are, the song's riff weaves around while the Farfisa keyboard, bass, drums and guitar stumble around in a style suggestive of the drunken, sad couple in the final scene of *Last Tango in Paris*. I can feel the shape and influence of a decade of listening to cynical punk wordsmiths like Elvis Costello, so in a way the song bridges the psychic worlds between the two Elvises in my imagination.

Lyrics have always transfixed me, both as a punter and as a creator, and never more than here. A jotter who learned his art of librettist as a child, improvising endless jazz-inspired stream-of-consciousness dot-to-dot strings of words to my brother's guitar noodling. Perhaps this is actually a song about my parents, my father perennially obscure and cold, fathering a succession of children, and the communal misunderstanding being passed on Ibsen-like to the tenth generation. Why write just a simple pop song when instead you can write a novella with music for wheels and a quick getaway?

The video, made by Peter Scammell, featured a bride in a wedding dress, pigs, and smashed and exploding domestic consumer durables, such as toasters and television sets, perhaps unintentionally an intimation of where we felt our career was heading to. 'Please Be Cruel' had the indignity of being the band's first flop single, reaching No. 50. It became a joke amongst us in the late nineties, that our singles compilation should be called *Inspiral Carpets Greatest Hits... and Please Be Cruel*.

### Born Yesterday

This was a collaboration between Graham, Martyn, Clint and myself. After we'd recorded the album, I went to a London gig where the rap band First Offence were playing, and I met the *NME* journalist Roger Morton. One of the jokes that revolved around the *NME* office was that Roger and Mary Anne Hobbs would make up for the parlous salary of music journalism by writing pornography for magazines. Crikey, I know which I would rather read! I told Roger that the song was about cross-dressing, which in fact it is; something hinted, but not expressly set out in the words. Roger gave the album a great review!

## *Sleep Well Tonight*

This is a song penned by Clint that was inspired by the first trip we made to Washington DC. An American friend took him to a park where he was introduced to some peace protestors who had been staging a sleep-in in a park near the White House to demonstrate against America's involvement in the Gulf War. This was first initiated as a month-long protest, but eventually flowered into a camping session of a few years. The song speaks of the political engagement of those Americans who register anger at their country's military foreign policy. It is a pacifist call to arms, encouraging soldiers to lay down their weapons, tear up their military papers and go AWOL – or at least it is a paean to political idealists who are bold enough to stand up for what they believe in.

## *Grip*

This song was first heard at the GMEX concert in 1990 and features on the video *21.7.90*, and then at the Reading Festival. Martyn wrote the beginnings of the song and I wrote the dour lyrics – end-of-relationship stuff, which may reflect an unhappy home life on my behalf. The music is funky A Certain Ratio-inspired garage rock, with staccato scratch guitar and big keys.

*Beast Inside*

Clint brought the thought-provoking words and bell chime samples into the rehearsal room. We then melted it down into our own brand of Nick Cave-ish brooding. Lyrically, the trip to Dachau in 1990 had greatly affected all of us, and nowhere is this influence felt more closely than in this song. So much so, that when the title *Never Again* was rejected, *The Beast Inside* was immediately chosen as the best title for this dark-themed album instead.

The end of the track has a vocal crescendo, which was a high point of the song. I really struggled to get the performance right in Ridge Farm. I had to re-record the vocal later in Stockport. Sometimes it is difficult to recreate the freshness of a vocal ad-lib in the captivity of a studio.

*Niagara*

This song was written by Graham, so the Marilyn Monroe film noir of the same name is surely of significance. It is a quiet, plaintive song, laid back and mournful with a lot of stoned reverb on the vocal. We were trying to move away from the brash garage pop of *Life* and move to a terrain more redolent of ambient experimental artists, such as Talk Talk and Philip Glass, a move many of our fans maybe didn't favour. I can hear a similar quiet silence and menace to 'Niagara' in songs by other artists, in PJ Harvey's song 'Catherine' for example.

*Mermaid*

During the recording of the album, Clint had been pursued by a young female fan, who famously chased him around in a basque, and it sounds as though this song may have been inspired by the experience; the mythical muse floating and splashing through our lives, the Balearic-inspired house-style piano runs, spinning like driftwood and starfish in the tide.

The cute pun on the band name with the line 'like a shell twists round in spirals' indicates the levity and light touch in the song, a pleasant sunny upland moment on a charnel house of an album, a breath of air amongst the self-enforced gloom.

*Further Away*
This was a monster psychedelic jam, born in the rehearsal room, and given its first outing at the 1990 GMEX show and then at the Reading Festival. The idea of the song germinated in me. I had read Tom Wolfe's *The Electric Kool-Aid Acid Test*, which refers to the activities of Ken Kesey and the Merry Pranksters; holding impromptu raves and drug parties and encouraging the local straights to 'tune in and drop out'. This book intersects nicely with *Hell's Angels*, a book by gonzo journalist Hunter S. Thompson, who actually got hospitalised by the Hell's Angels after publication for the way he portrayed them. Both books describe the Pranksters' odyssey across the States in a 1939 International Harvester bus named 'Furthur'. The song was intended to be a conscious quotation of the past and a communication across decades of the shared ideas of counter-cultural exchange through cultural weapons such as music, T-shirts, drugs, good times and sense of ribald humour. From the Pranksters' symbolic sharing out of psychedelic-laced orange juice, to our very own cultural Manchester experiment in what the *Face* magazine dubbed 'The Second Summer of Love'.

The song describes the arc of an accelerating fall, the very trajectory Lucifer makes in Milton's *Paradise Lost*. It is the sound of knife on bone, of the Scud missiles that Saddam Hussein toyingly arced towards Israel in the first Gulf War. We fed the live CNN newsfeed out of the television jack plug, rooted it through the 24-track desk and onto the track while mixing at Stockport's Strawberry Studios, because it was happening in real time and it seemed like a good idea.

*Dreams Are All We Have*

The closing track on the album was an instrumental. Clint utilised all the new sounds he had on his Akai sampler and Ensoniq VFX keyboard on this piece of modernism. I got irritated with the rest of the band all contributing to a track that I wasn't performing on. I felt excluded and was probably being a bit childish. As a joke, Chris Nagle recorded backing vocals by Clint and Noel, parroting the line 'Dreams are all we have. Dreams are all we have' over the main refrain. Eventually, when I had been publicly ridiculed by Clint at the playback for my self-possession, they admitted it was a joke and wiped the vocal tracks.

*The Beast Inside* was released on 7th May 1991, reaching an end-of-week chart position of No. 5. *The Beast Inside* was artistically a successful record, but in pop terms, the album's antennae were pointing in the wrong direction. We had misjudged our audience, making a record that wasn't the one that our youthful 'Madchester' followers had come to expect from us. We had made the mistake of trying to be too clever with our songwriting, perhaps the shift in political balance from having been truly independent running our own label through the distributor Nine Mile to having to work with Mute wasn't proving as easy as we had thought it might.

The album received mixed reviews, and it never sold all its original pre-release copies, a fate that befalls most bands at some time or another. You can tell albums that don't sell their initial pre-release shipping to record shops because, for years afterwards, you can find copies of said albums in all types of cheap retail premises, especially charity shops and cheap wallpaper stores, usually for a pound each.

We licked our wounds over the summer and autumn of 1991, and began the task, helped by both Daniel Miller and the staff of Mute, to first admit that we had dropped a bollock on *The Beast Inside*, and to then begin the process of focusing on writing for the next album. The decision to use Chris Nagle by the band as the producer was now universally accepted to have been the wrong choice. Ultimately, Inspiral Carpets making an album with our choice of producer allied with an inappropriate song selection had led to us getting 'too serious' and a desire on our behalf of wanting to be a proper dark Mute-style band had contributed to this multiple failing also.

To be fair on Chris, he was working with us at a difficult time. Having just come off a well-sold first album, we were a bit punch drunk from the success. It had been sometimes a little odd working with him at Ridge Farm. Chris was a diabetic and often Clint or Graham would have to enter the little cottage he was staying in at morning times and slap his face to rouse him from his sleep so that he could start work. The recording and mixing of the album sounds clunky to me and, in places I can hear 'drop-ins' – parts where a bit of vocal or instrument has been overdubbed, and the place where the join comes in can be heard. I don't blame Chris, he is a great producer, and when I met him at the launch for our following album at a club in London, he said to me, accusingly, 'Where were all the hits when I was recording your last album?' He had a point.

So dented was our collective ego by making a bollock-up of our second album that we all suffered a loss of confidence, especially Clint and Graham, which meant that, when the next album cycle came up, they weren't forthcoming in terms of forwarding material – so I stepped into the breach.

# 15

## Here's the rain, slip and slide in vain

We filmed the video for 'Caravan' in Almeria, Spain, on the old set where Sergio Leone's Spaghetti Westerns were filmed, and where Depeche Mode had made the video for 'Personal Jesus'. Martyn ate some dodgy prawns on the plane to Madrid and got food poisoning, which started frighteningly as a red-line rash that began at his wrist and worked its way to his torso. Clint was ill during filming and necking whole packs of Ibuprofen. He said the pills made his dick shrivel, which was more information than was strictly required.

About two hours into the day-long shoot we got bored with the filming and drove off against the moon-like mountainous terrain in the local production company's camper van. The van, incidentally, was the very same one that appeared in The Comic Strip's film *A Fistful of Travellers' Cheques*.

Once separated from the crew and director (who was still asking Clint to drive us back a quarter of a mile into shot) we drove on another mile, stopping near a cliff edge, and walked off some thirty yards from the van. Graham and Clint started to launch rocks from the ground towards the vehicle. Craig picked up a small piece and threw it over-arm from twenty yards. As it flew through the sky Graham posed quizzically in characteristic cricket-based style, as if asking 'Any chance for a run out?' The stone arched down and struck the camper van window squarely in the middle. For a nanosecond the glass seemed to hold, and we all went quiet, then the skin shook and the whole glass edifice exploded.

We all roared with the full-blown laughter of an emotional release – and my voice is very loud. Our collective reaction filled the craters and hillsides of the lunar landscape and I'm sure the crew would have heard it from where they were, even at that distance.

The director's voice through the walkie-talkie punctuated our laughter as we considered options and entertained the idea of avoiding the broken windscreen issue by pushing the thing over the cliff's edge, just for the sheer hell of it, and then claim that the handbrake had slipped and it had gone over the edge of its own accord. We realised that our bags were in the back and that we would have to explain why we had retrieved them before the van went bye bye, so instead we drove back to set. I suggested to Clint that we might distract the Spanish owner of the camper van from noticing the broken window by helpfully switching the wipers on double-fast speed, like some VW-inspired Don Quixote tilting at windmills. It didn't work, and the whole crew sat, silent and disgusted, through the lunchtime break of thin, chewy chicken.

'Caravan' reached No. 30 in the charts, which was a disappointing position given the expense of the video and considering that this was the lead-up single to the release of our second album.

# 16

## I'm moving on, you are right besides me

After we'd recorded *The Beast Inside* we set off on a North American tour. We stopped off first in Texas: Dallas and then Austin. At the Dallas show Clint got talking to twenty-year-old Meagan Sheehan – a beautiful girl who had attended the same college that Vanilla Ice had some years earlier. Clint seemed very much in love with her from the off. I think the rest of the band and crew thought that Meagan would not be someone we would see again in a hurry, but what we didn't know was that Meagan's mother worked as a member of the security staff for American Airlines. Meagan could therefore fly around North America for $15, which meant that she followed us around for many of the remaining shows, both on this tour and the following European tour. Still, you can't actually help falling in love, and it was a revolutionary time for Clint, as it was for the rest of us. It was the time of our lives.

This situation did raise tensions between the band members and crew though. Clint's other-/ex-girlfriend, Debbie, was back in the UK keeping the home fires burning and our office running. The Meagan situation felt like history repeating itself. Just as Debbie had caused the band problems in 1989 by travelling everywhere with us, we were now going through it all again.

The following excerpts are taken from a diary I wrote during the band's North American *Life* tour – our first album had just been released in the US through Elektra. These journals are a glimpse of what it was like on the road at the level of our day-to-day issues. As usual, I was a bit of a loner. Graham and Clint shared a room; Martyn and Craig shared a room; I stayed in singles.

## 1st March 1991: Denver, Colorado

Thirty-hour drive from Seattle to Denver, booked in hotel, washed, changed clothes, did phone interviews. Chilled around town, bought some books, Reeboks, Diesel black jeans. Met Mike from Elektra and the entire band went to the premier of the Oliver Stone film *The Doors*. It was really good. Came back to the hotel in order to have an important meeting with Mute's lawyer because we are arguing over the US deal.

## 2nd March 1991: Boulder, Colorado

Swim in the heated hotel pool. At 11am we drove to the campus where we are playing. Steve Rouson reversed the truck into a bollard, lucky it wasn't a boulder! Ha! Read letters from England, faxed mix suggestions to Chris Nagle. Met mad fan, half Chinese/half French called Cecelia. We drove overnight to Minneapolis, talked to the driver John about William Shakespeare.

## 3rd March 1991: Minneapolis, Minnesota

Reading Shakespeare's sonnets. Driving non-stop. We are now in a new time zone, we book into the hotel and I write twenty letters and postcards. We go to a Japanese restaurant, food cooked in front of us. Cold snow, Midwest feel. Coffee-making machine in my room, listen to the David Byrne and Brian Eno album, *My Life in the Bush of Ghosts*.

## 4th March 1991: Minneapolis, Minnesota- Day Off

We debate with Bruce Kirkland (Mute Records America boss) about second album's tracks. Went out with Jeff Skellen

(Liverpudlian roadie who we politely named 'seagull shit head' because his hair had greyed prematurely) to see a folk singer called Sara Hickman at the Fine Line Music Café, where we met a very famous A&R man and producer called Howard. Howard is rumoured to be the inspiration for Ian Faith, the character who is the cricket bat-wielding manager in the *Spinal Tap* film.

We went out to see Dr John play at the First Avenue club, which is the location for many of the live scenes in Prince's *Purple Rain* film. The concert was bluesy and really good; he played piano and guitar – how versatile. Beer and beer. Talked about songs with Jeff till 2:30am.

### 5th March 1991: Chicago, Illinois – Day Off

We arrive at the Ambassador hotel. The doorman is called Walter; he was friendly and is interested in learning how to play the drums and wants to speak to Craig about technique. Mansi's phone is not working. We look out the window at an external air-conditioning duct some way below, which was famously damaged by Led Zeppelin launching a sofa out of the eleventh floor balcony in 1977. This was just some of the estimated total of $23,000 of damage caused during their stay. The cover shot for Phil Collins' album *No Jacket Required* was photographed here. Hitchcock filmed here for some of the scenes in *North by Northwest*.

The hotel restaurant has beautiful French waitresses, but, it's a little snotty as a place, and there are no plugs for the bath or sink – to discourage one from having a wash? I do my usual trick of rolling up a plastic bag and ramming it down the plug hole so I can stop the water and have a bath. Bought a $1000 Italian suit from a shop called Jeruz and had my hair cut by an Italian girl called Marla who said she would come to our show tonight. A black lady washed my hair, the society still seems quite divided on racial lines as to what jobs different races do, which is a little odd and old fashioned. Some black 'shoeshine boys' petitioned me to have my shoes shined but I feel uncomfortable with it as it's a genuine old fashioned 'Jim Crow' thing and not a Disney tourist recreation (not that I would have it done even if it were postmodern!) I went to an Armani shop and got my shades fixed.

## 6th March 1991: Chicago, Illinois
Cabaret Metro show. Amazing concert, go down to the 'Smart Bar' downstairs with fans, but only eighteen-plus allowed in. Horrible bus journey, very bumpy, get no sleep. I want to get off the bus.

## 7th March 1991: Detroit, Michigan
Everyone is rude; ugly, concrete city connected to the General Motors building. Breakfast in Burger King, go to gig, eat pizza with Graham. Rude taxi drivers who mistakenly assume our accents to be Irish as it's soon to be the St Patrick's Parade.

The venue is a school concert hall, there was a bust of the founder which Clint drew eyes on with a permanent marker pen (v funny). A steam valve on a heating radiator was broken and emitting potentially scalding steam. Before the soundcheck, we have a major walk through the venue. A walk through the toilets takes you to another club and the dressing room isn't secure for possessions, so we don't use it. Another reason is that there is a record company tosser in it who keeps saying stuff like, 'I thought this was the hospitality bar.' There are eight fans outside who want to come into the soundcheck, but they seem a bit mad so we don't let them.

Outside the comfort zone of the gig in a northern district of the city, a man shot five people dead in a butcher's shop. (That will have Morrissey smiling!) Went for the slowest meal in the world in a Greek restaurant, pitchers of beer, lynch mobs and ham omelettes and onion rings.

The concert was very quiet, a bit like a soundcheck, a bit of a disappointment. We encore with 'Real Thing' and 'Biggest Mountain'. There is a fan in the audience wearing a Tottenham Hotspur scarf. We now have a very long drive over the border to Toronto; the border guards just wave us through and the boys stop at a pancake house.

Merchandise total for the tour is $4,500. Steve (Rouson) is charging loads for short-sleeve tops. Two videos have arrived by FedEx from the UK – the first one contains Clint's performance on *Star Test*, a Channel Four programme where celebrities are quizzed by a 'computer'. The second VHS is a new edit of the 'Caravan' video.

## 8th March 1991: Toronto, Ontario
Arrived at 9:30, time zone difference. 10:30 booked into hotel: washed, cleaned, slept till 17:00 then went to the gig. Mansi overslept, so all the crew did too. The sleeper bus broke down. Avoided interviews, soundcheck good. No toilet in the dressing room, so have to piss in four cups! Lights go off in the dressing room, so have to leave fridge door open to see. Concert great. 1000 people, trouble with all-ages show though. Tickets printed incorrectly making out that it is an all-ages show when it is for over 21s. Great reaction. Drive to Montreal. Snow outside. Good day.

## 9th March 1991: Montreal, Quebec
Felt rough in the morning, listened to Public Image Ltd – it sounded good while reading poems by Emily Dickinson as we drove through the Montreal streets. Arrived at 8:30 in the morning to find the original hotel overbooked, went to The Grand instead. The bus driver, John Schott, is enjoying himself in a particular redneck way by swearing at the

'Frenchies' over the CB radio. I offer him my Edith Piaff CD and we played 'Non, Je Ne Regrette Rien' down the CB channel, which didn't go down too well. This radio business evidently had the desired positive effect on the locals because Di and Ed suggested we go to a particular diner for breakfast. They got in the rear of two stationary cabs, but when we sat in the front cab and explained that the folk who knew the name and address of the fare were sat behind, the cab driver started shouting 'English fucks' and refused to drive us. So, a few slammed doors later, and we were eating breakfast in the hotel. We only have an hour or so before we have to be off to do some television interviews, so time is of the essence. Unfortunately, once we got in the hotel I got separated from the rest of the crew and couldn't remember the number of the day room. I used a phone on a stray landing and rang down to reception to try to establish the number. They were being really officious and threatened to get the security to throw me out of the hotel if I didn't come back down to the reception so, aware of the time, I found a freshly made-up room and dived in for a wash. I could see the hotel where Yoko Ono and John Lennon had their 'Love in', 'Sleep in' or 'Bag in' through the window. Did a TV and press interview with Clint, then another with CBC at the gig. Kentucky Fried Chicken, bad soundcheck, shit monitors. There is a Warner Music record company man here called Antonio.

Loucas, our lighting technician, tied the backdrop using the spare keyboard as an anchor. We did an interview with *TV With Claude* for a Canadian music channel called MusiquePlus. It's similar to Toronto's MuchMusic, which is a fiercely independent Canadian counterpart to MTV. Canadians don't want to be considered American, so a defiant stance against MTV by having your own cable channel is a sure way to guarantee success. Slept two hours on the sleeper bus from 7–9pm, then played. Problems overall, but good audience. After the concert, I was chatting to some French girls who had a bug up their arse about how, in their opinion, all the English universally love the Royal Family. I pointed out that we actually cut the head off Charles I in 1649, which is 144 years before the French did the same to Louis XVI and that the success of the Sex Pistols' 'God Save the Queen' might suggest such a generalisation incorrect. After the show we went back and washed in the day room, and then left the hotel and slept on the sleeper bus.

## 10th March 1991: Newhaven, Connecticut – Day Off

Went for a meal with Mansi and Jeff Skellen, drank beer called Taj Mahal. We had a conversation about the relevant benefits of vinyl and CD formats, analogue versus digital, and tits! Came back and watched *Lethal Weapon*, it was a shit edit for TV with the best bits removed. Wrote a letter to Alison and one to my sister Helen, loads of sleep and chilling out, nice to get the sleep and relaxation I won't be getting over the next ten days or so. Bought three films for my camera, took some pictures, spoke to Alison, nice conversation.

## 11th March 1991: Newhaven, Connecticut

Woke up this morning after at least sixteen hours sleep! Went down to the hotel restaurant and had fresh fruit and Raisin Bran. Spoke to Naney Black, a waitress, about Jamaica, where she is from. Collected washing from the Chinese laundry, had to wait for the dry cleaning. Went for spicy chicken and Cajun rice across the road from the hotel at a fast-food shop called Popeye's. Graham and Clint went to do an in-store (signing session) with Bonnie from NYC. I did a video interview with the *Vox Pops* comedy programme, with a comedian interviewing in character as an ageing English rock star called 'Nigel Cocktail'. Went to the gig at 4 o'clock, but no one there. Next to the gig was a bookstore where I bought a copy of Walt Whitman's *Leaves of Grass*, and Jane Austen's *Pride and Prejudice*. Wrote postcards back home to Mute, Mute International, and to Peter, Andrew and Vicky. We did a press conference where loads of college radio kids asked us all the predictable questions about the 'Manchester scene', other bands, Factory etc. Went for a meal with Bonnie, Jim and Brian, where we talked about sex and the occult and Happy Mondays. Did the gig, weird *Twin Peaks*-style audience. There was an Uncle Sam-type, 85-years old with a beard and an American flag at the front. Good performance of 'Further Away'. The bus broke down so we walked to the hotel, bought falafel with Jeff Skellen, and came back to the bus, then wrote this. '3AM Eternal' KLF!

### 13th March 1991: Boston, Massachusetts

Where is Binsey with a tape of the second album and the test prints of the cover artwork?

Arrived in the morning, woke after four and a half hours sleep. At 9:30 read a bit of *Dorian Gray*, then slept on until 12:15 (remarkable!). Mansi couldn't find me because he went to the wrong bunk on the bus. He got me up for an 'important' radio interview. Got up, washed, and ate at McDonalds (fruit and fish burger) all in the space of forty minutes.

Dried hair without a brush, met Jim and girl from Mute America, went to WNXY radio station with Martyn, then on to the local WEA distribution warehouse. Met a PA called Lisa from Atlantic and blagged loads of CDs from their offices. Went to gig, soundcheck good, but hurried, then went to meal in Thai restaurant – had soup with shrimps. Went with Clint, Mansi, Lisa and a friend called Cathy and talked about preoccupations. Marc Geiger, our agent from William Morris Agency, was also there and we talked about the tour.

The gig was great, the encore was 'Out of Time'. I walked all over the stage for a change. Talked to Elektra A&R man, Jon Leshay, getting ready for the big day. Chilled with the audience, signed T-shirts and records for Jeff on the merchandise stall. Talked to goth girls about Christina Rossetti and the Pre-Raphaelites. Groupie Doom. Heard a story about Lampy's (Loucas') sexual habits, but can't repeat it here.

<u>14th March 1991: New York City, New York</u>
Arrived at the hotel outside New York, washed, fed, ate chicken and rice and roast beef bagel. A guy called Benito chauffeured us à la Spinal Tap in an industry car to Elektra Records in the 75 Rockefeller Plaza building. Shelly Goldberg split us up into two groups for interviews – Martyn and me went to do the MTV *120 Minutes* indie show. We tried to negotiate with Shelly to ask the presenter, ex-Londoner Dave Kendal, to not make all the questions about the 'Madchester' scene and Happy Mondays. Happy Mondays are also signed to Elektra, and we don't want to spend the whole trip promoting them, rather than ourselves. Back with the chauffeur where I talked to Jon Leshay. We listened to our new album in the big boardroom in Elektra. We blagged lots of CDs, especially classical ones on the label Praxis, and they are posting them back to the UK for me. Went to a gig with Benito driving, and then fired him off. Irritating rock-chick women with a lot of jewellery, dressed too young, a bit fucked up. Good restaurant. Did the second MTV interview of the day, this time with Graham and Clint, where we are invited to talk about sex in the nineties and of course Manchester, basically all the stuff Martyn and me avoided in the earlier interview. The gig was a bit slow. Drove to the next gig, listened to final mixes of our second album *The Beast Inside*.

<u>15th March 1991: Philadelphia, Pennsylvania</u>
Wake up, wake up, get wash, chilled out in a nice city, contrast
to hubbub of NYC. South Street – arty and nice, the venue
is a little theatre. Buy Holly some books in a really nice-
looking bookshop. Hippies at the gig. Sleep before the show,
meet Theresa on the bus. (Theresa is an American fan who
followed us around the UK and did some work experience
in our management office.) She was wearing a Barbarella cat
suit. Concert okay, mellow. Power trips out, Ben (lighting
director) is suffering badly with his broken toe, which
is going black. Meet a hairy friend of The Chameleons'
guitarist Dave Fielding after the show. Chill on the bus, say
goodbye to Peter Wright and Ken from Mute.

<u>16th March 1991: Asbury Park, New Jersey</u>
Get to Asbury Park, seaside, decayed town, looks like
Southend or Brighton. Very polluted sea, the area never
recovered from the race riots in the sixties that followed
the assassination of Martin Luther King in 1968. The hotel
is the Berkley Suite. Go to a diner called Franks. Clint is
moaning on about the distances we are travelling. WEA
woman Andrea takes us to an in-store 50 minutes away. We
get lost on the way which is irritating. Fans Jim and Bonnie
there, bad tempers abound.

I get three CDs: Bauhaus, Beach Boys and *Closer* by Joy
Division. I drive to a toy shop and have a good conversation
with Bonnie about Mute's relationship with Elektra. Rest
of the band go to a radio interview. When I return, I walk
along prom and have a meal in a seaside restaurant, talk
about property prices in the village. I met Jen from NYC
who is getting drunk on Bailey's – Yuk! Club out of Hell,
girl fan gives us flowers, Latino fans Jose Nelson and Edwin
from Elizabethan (band) enthusiastic. The power goes off
during the soundcheck, they fix it. Gig at 12 o'clock. Go to

a yacht club with Noel, Mansi, Mark and Jeff, a dangerous van journey there then cab back. The gig was difficult, shit monitors. Chill after the gig. Move on.

## 17th March 1991: Washington, DC – St Patrick's Day

Arrive in a big city, plush hotel. Green beer dyed to celebrate St Patrick's Day. The Americans appear a little confused, trying to make an originally now-ruined Czech beer (Budweiser) Irish by dyeing it with green food dye. Theresa and her friend Katy bring chocolate brownies and a card for my baby, which is due in September. I go to an in-store with Graham in Georgetown, but there is no one there. (Kick my ass Artie Fufkin, another Spinal Tap moment. 'Kick my ass go on, kick my ass.') I meet a woman called Andrea who is into poetry and writing. I invite her to the show and go for an iced coffee where we talk about novels, writing and poetry. The café is in the gay part of town. We discuss Kylie Minogue and Oleta Adams with her friend Felice. The club is the downstairs of an old variety style theatre. Call Alison reverse charge from the phone in the club's hall. She tells me that Liam Walsh had her printing Inspiral Carpets T-shirts, and a meeting with her bank manager went well for her clothing business. Soundcheck late! Go to McDonalds with Clint, meet fans from Pennsylvania. Hang out with Theresa and a woman called Kym from New Zealand on the bus. The concert is good, with Mark Coyle shouting 'bollocks' through the monitors throughout the concert. Voice is good – pleased. We played at the 9:30 Club which seems amazingly small. Talked to Theresa after the show, read poetry and got pissed with Mark. Stop at 4:00am for burger.

## 18th March 1991: Atlanta, Georgia

Listen to the *Soundtracks* album and *Closer* while reading Andy Warhol's *Interview* magazine, which has pieces by

Hunter S. Thompson and Danny Sugarman speaking out against censorship. Arrive at 1:00pm, have been travelling for eight hours. Get to the hotel, which is called the Colony Square. Empty everything on the bed and sort it all out, washing and dry-cleaning. We take whiskey and beer from the bus. In the room, a big open window, and sunny. Say goodbye to the bus driver, John Schott. He says he is off to sleep on a waterbed! Jon Leshay rings up, he is in town, wants to go out for a meal. Jeff and me go out with him to an Italian restaurant. The cab driver is mad, he seems drunk, drives around without the headlights switched on, and is obsessed with the TV chef Keith Floyd, probably because he visited Atlanta to make a BBC programme about Cajun-style cooking and was a regular fare of the driver. Also, he is the nearest point of reference that he has to our Englishness; we must seem very sober in comparison. Leshay bullshits the cabbie and tells him we are a gospel choir from Manchester, UK, mischievously called Happy Mondays. I call Lisa at Baylis and Knight to arrange for some flowers and chocolates for Alison because she is a little down.

Jonathan Pernick and Faith from NY come, and Melanie, a weird denture-ridden witch-type, comes drinking tequila. Got boshed. Drive to Jon's hotel to pick up some grass – then on to the Gold Club. It's a titty bar with girls in massive Mexican hats and belts with a lot of shot glasses set in them, walking round the club selling shots of tequila, of which we have many. We watch women and drink Bushmills. Jon buys me a table dance from one of the girls, and I blush, embarrassed, while she dances. They find this shyness hilarious, of course. After talking to them, it turns out most are single mums, earning money for their kids or to get through college. I invite a couple of the dancers to tomorrow's show. I am introduced to a Poodle Rock band called Nelson who are made up of two of Ricky Nelson's sons, Matthew and Gunnar. I tell them that their hair looks ridiculous. This doesn't go down very well. Go back to the hotel, very drunk, make a request to the radio station to play 'Could You Be Loved' by Bob Marley. Jon requests 'This Is How It Feels'. Jeff makes his own way home.

## 19th March 1991: Atlanta, Georgia
## Room 904, Colony Square

Wake up hungover, feeling weird. Drink water, go to plaza for a coffee, and some kind of hot food I can't recall! Jeff gets up at 1:00pm. Plaza again, tuna and chicken mayo sandwich. Both still drunk from previous night. I think the tequila may be stuck in our stomachs and the liquid is diluting it again and sending it spinning helplessly around our blood streams. Sit in the hotel room listening to Ella Fitzgerald album, with songs like 'The Hunter Gets Captured by the Game', and Jimi Hendrix's *Axis: Bold as Love*, and Jeff's bootleg live cassette. Feel chilled as we watch men painting a building on the opposite side. The room is a total tip. Leshay calls (totally unnecessarily) to apologise for previous night's behaviour. Jeff has lost his jacket and can't remember how he got back from the club, and of course now doesn't have his passport, which was in the pocket. Graham and I go to a radio station to do an interview. Russian Roulette with the CD player where the DJ puts our album on random and we don't know which song will be cued up! Go to the gig at the Cotton Club where there is tension with the crew. The soundcheck goes well. Go to Chinese to meet Elektra knobs and local radio and TV channel people, go to the hotel and chill. The gig is empty, play set humorously with Mark Coyle again shouting 'bollocks' down the monitors and singing bits of songs by REM at the end of 'Out of Time'. Clint dances on the drum riser, we make lots and lots of mistakes, probably due to the lack of nerves induced by the lack of an audience.

I sip iced tea after the show and stay off the drink. Go for a pizza with Craig, where they are playing Led Zeppelin. Good food, and the place has a great set of kitsch pictures of historical greats, such as J.F. Kennedy and Jackie, and rugs and a clock which has a picture of the last supper. I get an early night.

### 20th March 1991: Atlanta – Home

Martyn wakes me up at 10:30am with a phone call. I organise my suitcase and wash. Jeff is fucked, bad hiccups, he came in at 4:00am swearing and kicking the door. Get shit together, try to pay the incidentals on the room, but they are too big, so I give in and get the band to pay for them. Go to Lennox's Mall with Di Barton and Jeff, have a club sandwich and then we go for a coach ride through beautiful trees and wooden houses in a Waltonesque mountainscape. Buy a Harley Davidson T-shirt and Pink Floyd album, *The Piper at the Gates of Dawn*, go back to the hotel. Everyone in room 918 is crashed, go to airport with an aggressive driver. Wait at the airport, get on the plane and write this diary up.

# 17

## On a white knuckle ride

*The Beast Inside* was released on 7th May 1991. The following extracts are taken from my diary, written during a European tour to promote the album. While touring in Europe, the crew had their own tour bus exclusively for their use, whereas we travelled by plane then took up our own bus, before getting rid of it because the driver was unacceptable, and getting yet another bus and driver.

<u>9th May 1991: Hamburg, Germany</u>
Fly From Manchester to Düsseldorf, then on to Hamburg via Lufthansa. Craig, Martyn and me pick up the food for the second flight in a bag. Clint and Graham are in Oslo doing promotion with Fad Gadget (Frank Tovey) and will be joining us in Hamburg. We arrive at the airport as usual and my small 'club' bag has gone missing in transit, probably when we changed planes in Düsseldorf. I speak to Alison and then on to the Marriott Hotel. Only 500 tickets sold for the gig. All the crew are here, including Paul and Wilf who are our on-tour caterers. During the soundcheck we start moving the set order of the songs around, which enrages the lighting crew. There is a rumour that Osman Eralp, the Turkish American entertainment consultant who helped set up the Mute/Elektra deal, is staying at our hotel to talk to us about how *The Beast Inside* is doing. I am trying to chase my missing bag, which luckily is relatively easy to sort out. Sleep before the gig. Show starts at 8:30pm, all the audience

stays sat down, which is a bit disconcerting to any performer who isn't expecting it. They are appreciative though, which makes up for them sitting down. The encore is 'Out Of Time' and 'Skidoo'. Daniel Miller came backstage, annoyed that we didn't play the show stopper 'Further Away' – he must like it and has bigged it up to the music industry folk he brought with him. Not playing 'Further Away' is perhaps a bit of a gaffe on our behalf. Erik van Kassen from Mute Records' German licensee, Intercord, has come along with another German called Peter, who is their head of A&R, and who appears to be a total pisshead, unlike Erik who's a good bloke. Craig and Martyn go to the club upstairs while I go back to the hotel and have food in the room, which is chicken and chips, but I have a major problem explaining what a pot of tea is. I watch a weird programme on the 'Super Channel' called *Blue Night*, where they talk about the associations of numbers. Read Walt Whitman's *Leaves of Grass,* make a phone call to Alison about cutting her clothing business down in size severely to meet the recession that is happening, then sleep.

## 10th May 1991: Brussels, Belgium

Woken by a call in the hotel saying that the airline have found my bag. The concierge delivers it to my room. We fly out after breakfast via a cab with Graham, Martyn and Clint. The female driver looks like Bet Lynch from *Coronation Street*. It's confusing to sort the fare as none of us have enough Deutschmarks to pay, so we have to pool all we have; a bit unsatisfactory really. We fly to Brussels; I sit next to Mansi on the plane. We arrive and book into the hotel where I phone Pete Donaldson, who says that Gary Clail from the On–U Sound System will be supporting us at Alexandra Palace for the big gig there over the summer. I listen to Can's *Delay 1968,* especially 'Thief', and *Songs for*

*Drella* by Lou Reed and John Cale, the album inspired by Andy Warhol's life, career and death. I sleep for two hours, go to the gig, same old Ancienne Belgique. Binsey is there, and he is still trying to get Blur to support us in Glasgow SECC and Manchester GMEX – he is on the mobile phone all the time. The soundcheck was easy. Craig is complaining about people putting graffiti all over the venue's white walls, which, after a few years of him doing similar stuff, seems a bit ironic to me. Went back to the hotel and listened to New Order, tried to call Alison but she wasn't in. The concert is at 8 o'clock. Someone had written 'Who is the biggest cunt in Manchester? _ _ _ _ _ _ / _ _ _ _ _' in permanent marker on a mirror. (Implying Binsey Smith.) Sounds as if the crew have got it in for Clint and Meagan, as she has turned up to follow Clint around Europe! Oh Lordy. Grief from the promoter to go on slightly later at 8:30, didn't talk to the audience, and went off early. Mansi and Binsey were concerned about the audience being disappointed. There were fans shouting 'refund'. Bruce Kirkland and Peter Wright from Mute America were in the dressing room with idiots from the European label, Play it Again Sam, who were trying to say that Inspiral Carpets' sole motivation for choosing Chris Nagle as the producer of *The Beast Inside* was to make us sound more like The Charlatans, because he produced their debut album (total bollocks!).

Talked business to Bruce about the forthcoming US tour. Surprise surprise! When I came back to the hotel there was loads of tension between the 'Engine Room' (Martyn and Craig) and the two Boons. I'm in the middle of it all! Tried to call Alison, but she was at the reopening of the Haçienda, so I left an answerphone message. Phoned her later and got through at 2am. I argued with her about money and how much she should spend on a new car stereo. Clint is in the process of buying a house in Milnrow, near Rochdale. Brian

Smith, the mortgage guy, is flying out on Monday to get his signature on the documents. Sleep.

## 11th May 1991: Cologne, Germany
Woke up and tried to have breakfast in the hotel, but it wasn't possible. Went to a snack restaurant, had jambon omelette and a hot chocolate. When we went back to the hotel, the van that had been hired turned out to be not big enough to transport the whole band, it was just a Renault Espace, so I opted to go by train to Cologne from the Gare du Nord. To Cologne: no buffet, irritating bearded man on the train. I ignored him, sat opposite a nun and started *Don Quixote* and listened to Smokey Robinson. The train stopped three times, once in Aachen, then at Düren. The first thing I saw when I got to Cologne was the beautiful GMEX-type station which I last saw when I was visiting Tracy seven years ago, and the gothic cathedral. Got a cab to the Ramada Renaissance hotel. We went for a pizza with Mansi. Noel had a Weizenbier. There were arguments about whether Meagan should be allowed on the crew bus. Clint saw a V-Max at some traffic lights, which is his favourite motorbike. He explained to Graham and me all about it. Lots of porn shops with fairly hard-core material, pissing videos and the like. I was feeling a little drunk when a middle-aged bald bloke approached us, saying that he had interviewed us two months before, which was embarrassing because we had all blanked him. Oldham Athletic won the league. Went to see Mark Coyle and spoke to Loucas about the lighting and how he got into being a lighting director. Went back to my room and read *Don Quixote*.

## 12th May 1991: Cologne, Germany – The E Work
On the way to the gig there were bridges with cable cars over them. The concert took place in an industrial estate

115

two or three miles out of town, a bit like Trafford Park in Manchester. Ed the monitor man was back from the Happy Mondays' tour of the United States. In the dressing room, Graham took his top off and rubbed cream cakes from the food rider into his bare chest, which was funny and a little manic and scary. The concert was alright. After the show we were talking to six security guards and two fans. A fan wanted us to sign his poster, so Graham took it off him and teased him by pretending to sign it. Then we stole the van from Mansi and Clint started driving around the car park, while a little pissed. He drove it in a crazy way, talking as if he was a criminal being chased by Starsky and Hutch. Eventually we let Mansi get back in, but it was funny. Mansi kept on getting lost on the way back to the hotel, which we naturally responded to by being supportive in a none piss-taking way! Craig stayed on the tour bus with the crew while we went back to the hotel. Mansi of course found that he still had Craig's passport, so we had to drive all the way back to the gig again. Happy days! Graham, Martyn, Clint and me stayed up drinking Weizenbier. Martyn and Clint went to bed and Graham and Mansi stayed up and talked about football teams of the seventies. I talked about John Donne with Mansi, and went to bed.

13th May 1991: Amsterdam, The Netherlands. The Paradiso
Got up, drove to Holland. Graham is covered in bags in the back of the Renault Espace to make enough room for us all to get in. Mansi tells us that he doesn't like Amsterdam, especially the hippies who run the Paradiso. We stopped at a petrol station and had a kick around. A hard-core pornographic magazine was bought from the petrol station; it had a woman dressed up in PE kit, being done by three men. Mansi couldn't find his way to the Leidseplein. Eventually we directed him to the American Hotel, and we drove past

the Rijksmuseum on the way. Arrived at the venue. I didn't want to leave my bags and leather jacket in the Espace because I was worried that the vehicle would get broken into – there are a lot of heroin addicts in Amsterdam. Walked around the venue and went on the bus. Oz (sound man) was really pissed off because someone had left the tour bus unlocked and a load of bags were stolen. Paul the caterer has lost £3000 in cash and traveller's cheques and all his clothes, a bit depressing – all goes to show that benefit of hindsight is useless. Adam from Manchester band The Train Set was outside the venue with his girlfriend. The Train Set's 'She's Gone' is one of Noel 's favourite songs; he used to have the song on a compilation cassette that he brought on tour with us in 1989. The soundcheck is good, the venue has high ceilings and stained-glass windows. I go and check a record shop, then go to a sportswear shop with Martyn, and he talks about how he thinks that his girlfriend Joanne might be pregnant. We didn't discuss the Clint and Meagan situation. Manchester United are playing Barcelona in Rotterdam tomorrow so we may have some Manchester fans in the gig tonight! We play the gig to about 700 people, it is a respectable show and for the first time on this European tour we loosen up a bit. The tour bus for the band arrives; a man called Peter Best, a cockney, not the ex-drummer of The Beatles, is driving it. He is a bit of a cockney cunt and the bus it too posh for us; Clint gets a bunk that has a sunbed built in to it! Pete Best looks a bit like the darts player Eric Bristow. He shows us the 'visitors' book' for the bus – The Monkees, New Kids on the Block, and MC Hammer have all been on. Inspiral Carpets appear to be very unimpressive to Pete Best, and that appears to be affecting the way that he is treating us – a bit strange considering we are paying him £500 a day to at least be okay with us. Pete Best bollocks Craig for putting his coat on one of the seats, saying that it will damage the leather, before telling us how great Status Quo are. Snore, snore. No one likes Pete Best, we all think he is a cunt, irrespective of how many shit bands he has had on his bus.

Pete Best refuses to park the tour bus anywhere near the venue and parks it a fifteen-minute walk away behind the Rijksmuseum and near the Van Gough museum. The whole band visit a whorehouse, everyone goes in apart from me as I'm too embarrassed. Everyone comes out apart from Clint. We wait for him for twenty minutes, but it turns out that he has come out the back of the place and made his way back to the bus. We drive on to Frankfurt, but I can't sleep – the bunk is too claustrophobic. Paul the caterer and Ed go home to the UK. There was a national strike in the Netherlands because a driver was murdered today.

## 14th May 1991: Frankfurt, Germany

Wake up in Frankfurt and recognise the venue from the 1990 European tour we did, and the sound of the trains, which run next to it. Get up and breakfast on big fat German sausages. Steve Cannel, the merchandise man, is cooking for us now that Paul the caterer has gone home in order to stop anyone from cashing the traveller's cheques. Steve doesn't know where any of the stuff is, so the cooking takes quite a long time. Wilf, the other caterer, has gone out to buy provisions for this evening's meal. Have a wash in the venue's bathroom, which is difficult because it is small and dirty. I go and do all the band's washing in a launderette. I buy far too much washing powder. There is a hippy skinning up and smoking in there. I talk to the venue's runner about neo-fascists in Berlin, and the compromise between West and East Germany, and Chancellor Kohl's current unpopularity. There is a weirdo at the launderette who talks to me and says, 'Everyone here is an arsehole.' I come back after drying everything, which took ages. Pete Best has tried to ruin the suspense of watching the Manchester Utd game by telling us the result, which was them losing to Barcelona by 3–1. Cunt. By the time I get back to the venue, everyone has soundchecked. We play the B-side 'The Wind Is Calling Your Name' for the first time and it sounds really good. The monitors are rubbish, really weak and quiet. Before the show there is a queue that goes right around the bus! We play the concert, it is okay, but the audience reaction is a bit quiet perhaps. The audience all look as though they are dressed up to look like the singer from EMF – sad bastards! I talk to Binsey over the phone about trying to persuade Mute that Janice and Mel don't need to come with us to Milan and Athens. He doesn't seem convinced, though, and wants to keep Mute on side. Our agent from Primary Talent, Nigel Hassler, comes to see us at the gig and suggests that the support for the GMEX gig should be ex-Factory Records band The Railway Children and a Scottish band called The Apples should support us at SECC. Our bus drives on in convoy with the crew bus, we watch Man Utd thrash Barcelona on video. Martyn is going mad as the goals go in, Graham, who is an Oldham Athletic fan, throws his underpants around the bus; they land on the driver's head of course. I sleep, although in the excitement of the football match, no one else can.

<u>15th May 1991: Berlin, Germany</u>
Driving through East Germany over Hitler's original autobahns, which are now very bumpy roads on the corridor between what was formerly East and West German farmland. We see aged labourers pushing wheelbarrows of potatoes over the autobahn while BMWs barely miss them, driving past at 100mph. Gypsies with donkeys and tack riding down the side, sheer madness. We see the old checkpoint, now disused and stoned by children, I guess. Drive into the city,

Pete Best misses loads of turns, goes to the wrong Potsdamer Strasse, does four U-turns, eventually we get to the venue. We eat at the venue, the production office doubles as the catering room. Craig, Clint and Martyn go shopping, Graham and me go and have a look at the Brandenburg Gate and trace the path of *Die Mauer* (the Wall). I go to Potsdamer Platz where I was when I stayed with Tracy and busked on the Kurfürstendamm. I trace the section of Potsdamer Platz which was no man's land, where the old train lines ran under the wall and the observation towers rose menacingly above, and rabbits played over the space where Hitler's bunker had been.

A discarded Trabant lies abandoned at the side of the wall. We see a plant, which is cleverly recycling the wall by grinding the concrete into substrate, which is then compressed into blocks on site to manufacture as materials for the city's new flats in situ. We walk down to the Reichstag, which is now naked of the wall, and you can trace bullet holes in the buildings, which gives a sense of the dying days of the fight for Berlin. We walk back to Potsdamer Platz where we see people bungee jumping from a crane. This daredevil act is a metaphor for the new unified nation, the plunging down and the propulsion of the body upwards expressing the individual's right to taste danger; an utter rejection of the former Soviet state's crushing safety net. Scares the shit out of us when we see someone falling and being caught at the last moment by the rope and slung back up by the momentum and weight of the slack. Go to the venue then chill in the hotel around the corner. Mansi is under a lot of stress due to keeping on track with the tour budget and the unsuitability of Pete Best's tour bus. He loses it, and smashes his mobile phone up. Mansi has booked our tickets to Greece in our *Twin Peaks* nicknames. Play gig, Irish girls come backstage and sing 'Silent Night' to us with jealous boyfriends in tow, which is funny. Sarah Claughton comes backstage begging for food. (Sarah was an über fan who first followed Inspiral Carpets around our UK gigs in 1989, and then started following us around Europe.) We were concerned about her because she was travelling solo around our gigs, and we didn't want anything bad to happen to her. We fuck off into the night, down south to Munich along bumpy East German roads. Sleep, but drunk.

## 16th May 1991: Munich, Germany

Finally get to Munich, book into the Marriott Hotel, which is really nice. I stay in bed till 2pm, then buy postcards and write to Alison and Holly and various Inspiral Carpets fans. The concert venue is in an industrial estate. This time the concert is great. We play 'The Wind Is Calling Your Name' during the encore; there are loads of mad Germans at the front of the audience hitting cow bells and shaking maracas and wood blocks, they collectively really vibe the atmosphere of the gig up. Craig kicks Graham's Gibson SG across the stage at the end of the gig, not really sure why, but it looks good. Martyn has to take a piss at the beginning of 'Born Yesterday'. Clint starts the song anyway, which is a weird thing to do as it has a sixteen-bar drum and bass intro. We met all the record company knobs afterwards. Moaner is there, I have a bit of a flirt with her and joke with everyone back at the Marriott and catch some sleep. We have to get up at 6:30am to catch a plane to Athens. We had a meal with Schmidt and his girlfriend and Erik. Goodbye Germany.

## 17th May 1991: Athens, Greece

The tour bus takes us to the airport. We fly Austrian Airlines to Vienna. It's a foggy flight and the Austrians clap nervously once the pilot has completed the landing, which is worrying to us Brits. Catch a bit of sleep as the plane continues on to

Athens. It is a long flight. When we arrive at Athens airport all the gear gets searched, which is tiresome and we take a beat-up old bus to the hotel, which goes at about 3mph.

The hotel is alright. Chill out, speak to Alison, then with Kent (Head of Mute International). He is sounding reconciliatory about our concerns about Janice and Mel coming, I think we feel they are a bit bossy and too quick to tell us how to do interviews and behave, which we don't like, although they are top people. We do a ridiculous press conference where we get asked about T-shirts and Shaun Ryder. I squash both subjects firmly. We go out for a meal and I have really nice calamari and talk to a Greek lad about the Greeks versus the Turkish. Get a good sleep and chill out. I have a conversation with a Virgin Greece man about the Stranglers gig at the club we are playing, Club Rodon. It's their first show with new singer Paul Roberts, as Hugh Cornwell has left them to go solo.

### 18th May 1991: Athens, Greece. Club Rodon, first night
Get up, have toasted sandwich downstairs in the hotel. Interviewers turn up; we go for an impromptu photo session in the park over the road where we play with wild cats around the fountains. Graham and I go to the local radio station, Antenna 97.5, to do a one and a half hour interview with well-known indie radio DJ, Yannis. He plays 'This Is How It Feels', 'Please Be Cruel' and 'Mermaid', and talks straight over each of the songs. He then plays 'Stand By Me' by Ben E. King as my favourite record. We watch international news being read. Yugoslavia appears to be disintegrating in a post-Communist civil war (settling of scores), which locally has serious implications for the self-determination of Macedonia, which Serbian Nationalists want ceded back from Greece. We talk to top fans outside the station, and then go back to the hotel and chill.

I sit in the room and write postcards, then go out and buy an ice cream from a kiosk. At 4:30pm I go to the gig; it is a nice venue. I argue that with Greece being a relatively poor country and the ticket price being the equivalent of £9, that we should offer value for money by playing a slightly longer set than Germany, so we rehearse the songs previously dropped from the set including 'Sackville' and 'Move'. The soundcheck goes well, despite the keyboard amplifier being pretty much useless, and the rest of the backline gear fairly primitive. The promoter seems nervous about the show, and I do my best to reassure him. Alex (promoter's runner) takes us to a restaurant where we drink loads and get merry. The food is nice, and we go to the gig, fired-up in a van. The concert is really good. Appreciative audience, flamenco and Balearic style clapping along to the funk beats that Craig is supplying. I let a lad at the front sing some lines from 'Born Yesterday', which freaks the rest of the band out (good!). There is loads of dancing and it becomes a pass-the-mic competition like *The Hit Man and Her*.

On the drive back to the hotel, the drunken promoter kept trying to cut up our old bus with his sixties Triumph sports car, standing up while driving. Clint stuck his head out of the bus window shouting 'Peasants'. (The promoter had a crash later that night where I am convinced that he either seriously injured or killed someone.) After the gig, we go to a club with Alex, and we have to wait for an age for Mark Coyle to have a wash, then Mansi does a bunk. We argue with Alex, who takes us to a metal club where they play Modern Romance and the drinks are the equivalent of £15 each – ouch! It turns out that Alex deliberately took us to the wrong club as a joke to see the reaction on our faces when they played Elvis Presley covers and Modern Romance. The layout of the club makes the Haçienda seem like the Queen Vic from *EastEnders*. We go on to a house club, which is excellent, dancing away until it closes. Onto the next with sophisticated people, dance till 6am then walk back to the hotel with Martyn – what a day! The best on the tour yet! Go back to my room and listen to the Tracy Chapman album.

## 19th May 1991: Athens, Greece. Club Rodon, second night

Get up at 1pm to get some food, argue with the man at the kiosk because he wants to give me old pizza and I'm not having it. Walk about a bit then get a club sandwich at the hotel and chat to the woman who is serving, and put her brother on the guest list for tonight. I sleep a bit more until 4pm, then go to the venue where I play football in the car park with Alex, Mansi, Craig, Mark and Graham – good fun. In the soundcheck we try the song 'Niagara' from *The Beast Inside*. Judith Sanderson, a school friend from Abingdon, rings me up. (Judith got chucked out from John Mason School for dealing cannabis. I slept with her during a summer holiday in Dawlish in 1982 after riding pinion on her motorbike around the place. She was the inspiration for the first single I recorded with my band, Too Much Texas, 'Hurry on Down'.) I put her on the guest list. No one from the band went for the meal with Virgin. There weren't as many people at the concert tonight, though the audience were still mad. Clint took his Ensoniq synthesizer to the front of the stage and played it right up front for 'Further Away' during the encore, and about fifteen people were playing it. At the end, Craig kicked the drum kit over and the crowd were going crazy for it! After the concert, some people came backstage to the dressing room, which is high above the stage, up a steep flight of stairs. Judith and Micos came back to the hotel and we stayed up till 4am when I threw them out.

## 20th May 1991: Milan, Italy

Packed up, had a club sandwich downstairs, jumped on a

minibus and went to the airport, where the security were doing spot-checks on people. We flew on a horrible seventies plane with no overhead lockers, and it felt pretty unsafe. I slept a little and read the *Observer* newspaper. There was a ropey landing in Milan. Got to the baggage terminal and the sniffer dogs picked Mark Coyle out and he was searched. The guard said, in heavily Italian accented English, 'My dog says you have drugs.' Mark responded in thick Mancunian, 'Your dog's a liar then.' They let him go eventually.

The driver isn't at the airport when we arrive, so we get some expensive cars to take us into Milan; the cars race one another. I book into hotel room 16, horrible, so I change it, but even my new one has blinds that won't close. I get two hours sleep, and then we go out with Franco and Anthony from the record company to the nearby Buga and Fabio restaurant, then we go by underground to a club to watch The Fall perform. The record company had given us some large inflatable sausage-shaped balloons which had 'Inspiral Carpets' written on the side. Noel went right up to the front of the audience and started pushing and hitting and sticking one in Mark E. Smith's face; it was hilarious. There were about 150 punters there. We take the tube back to the hotel. I call Alison and she tells me that The Stone Roses have won their court case against Silvertone and are now free to pursue a new recording contract with a new company. Big news. Good for them!

21st May 1991: Milan, Italy. Rolling Stone
Woke up at 9:30am, thought that Mansi had forgotten to get my CDs off the bus before he got rid of it. I call Graham who tells me that Craig had them. We went to the offices of the Italian record company – they are very stylish and cool – and nearby is a very beautiful covered market. At the offices we watched the video for the new single, 'Please

Be Cruel'. It's really good and doesn't need the re-edit we thought it might need. I did four interviews while everyone else went shopping. Went to the venue; it's really nice and has about a 1000 capacity. The soundcheck is a bit grim, but I don't complain. Ate mental bacon, egg and tomato sauce sandwiches, went back to the hotel, washed my socks and pants in the sink, and talked to Tony English at Russells about our merchandising deal for ages. I reckon that he should conduct the negotiations. Couldn't speak to Alison, Paul was at home (Holly's dad). He told me that Alison had gone to view a house with her workmate, Bruce Atkinson. I told Paul about Holly getting hit at school by a child called Dmitry. Back to the venue in cabs, the gig was okay, about 400 in – polite, but nice. We end with 'The Wind Is Calling Your Name'. Tim Booth came backstage; we were flirting with mad Italian girls, gave them autographs too, he came back to the hotel to pack bags and go to sleep. I argued on the phone with Alison about whether she should come and visit us in Barcelona.

## 22nd May 1991: Rimini, Italy

Come down, get in the minibus and drive to Rimini. It's quite a nice drive through the Italian countryside. On the motorway we make a tinny and smoke some hashish. The police stop us for absolutely nothing. I argue with Graham about leaving the window open. We arrive in Rimini and there are loads of Africans in robes. The driver is grumpy and tries to take the bus under a low railway bridge that would have ripped the roof and our heads off, but we shout at him to prevent it. We arrive at the hotel – Carlton-by-the-Sea, really sunny and beautiful. Graham buys a volleyball and we go on the beach for a game of '60 Seconds', which I really enjoy (a game where you have to keep the ball in the air for a minute). Clint throws the ball to a dog on the beach, it catches it with its canines and punctures it. We all laugh as the air farts out. We decide to revise our travel plans and instead of driving, we'll fly to Switzerland the day after the gig, to give us an extra day in Rimini on the beach soaking up the sun. We go to the concert at 4pm, it's an old pizza restaurant/brothel, which traded in the Fascist period, and has been continuously open since. It's called Perestroika; nice vibe outside where we are playing on a stage in the garden. Soundchecked, the speakers are uneven, go back to the hotel where I listen to Ella Fitzgerald, then drive to the gig, no one there apart from a few female English students. Gig very quiet, encore with 'Further Away'. Martyn is angry with the rest of the band, saying we didn't put enough effort into the performance. Graham somehow loses his shoes.

<u>23rd May 1991: Rimini, Italy. Day Off</u>
Clint decides to go with the crew bus to Switzerland with Meagan, and in the process annoys the crew again by throwing one of them off their bunk and moving their possessions. The crew retaliate by throwing some of Clint and Meagan's stuff off the bus. Mark carries Clint's ghetto blaster around, and manages to lose the back of the battery cover, but doesn't really care less about it. Not wise to make yourself unpopular with your crew, I reckon. Have breakfast with Graham downstairs. We realise that the hotel is nearly empty due to it being out of season. Go on the beach and find a replacement ball after getting some lira. Play '60 Seconds' again with Martyn, Mansi and Graham. Craig is ill, going down with a cold. We have a pizza in a restaurant opposite the hotel then chill out in the evening, go to a taverna and have a drunken meal and pay in dollars from the Milan promoter. Sit in the bar looking at two football matches on the TV, simultaneously with MTV. There are posters of The Clash and The Stone Roses on the wall. Go

back to the hotel and finish off the skunk with Craig. We watch a thunderstorm over the sea. The lightning is striking the sea in impossible snaking patterns, a multicycle goes past with people on it, very surreal-stoned.

## 24th May 1991: Fribourg, Switzerland
Get up at 5:30am, go to Rimini airport, fly to Rome in a tiny plane with about eleven people in it. We change at Rome for another plane which takes us to Zurich. When we land, we meet the new band bus and two drivers called Paul and Pete. The bus is a vast improvement on the Pete Best bus – it's nice and I sleep for three hours on the way to the venue. The venue has terrible murals of famous musicians on its exterior. My throat feels worse, taking loads of Benilyn. Martyn and Graham also have colds and coughs. The concert is good and I freak out on stage. Graffiti in the dressing room says 'Carter USM'. We meet Bert from the Swiss record company, who is cynical about the likelihood of success of *The Beast Inside* in Switzerland. After the show we drive on for twelve hours to Barcelona.

## 25th May 1991: Barcelona, Spain
Wake up at 9.15am on the bus and talk to Paul, the driver – he seems like a nice bloke. We travel through a lot of toll roads, and I pass his credit card to pay the toll through the passenger window so he doesn't have to get out of his seat because the bus is right-hand drive. We drive through the Languedoc region, a barren part of France where they grow grapes for Fitou wine. We arrive in Barcelona at 12 o'clock, and check into the Regente Hotel. The lift isn't working and I lose my temper. Nice hotel, room 308 backs onto a courtyard. Alison and Karen (Graham's girlfriend) arrive at 3pm while I am in the bar. Alison looks healthy, but very pregnant. There has been a noticeable change in the two weeks since I last saw

Harry Wyatt and my grandmother. Peking.

My paternal grandmother.

My mother in China with a
broken fan.

Mother and Father's wedding day.

My brothers sat on the steps at Frilford Grange. Vicky in a flammable pram.

I want to be left alone. Blenheim Palace.

I made you laugh.

Raising funds for the church roof.

Brothers Andrew and Martin.

The local vicar's son.

Above Top: Me in Captain Mouldy
helmet with Will Rayson

Above: Debbie Keeping, Vicky, me,
Helen in the background

Ash Tray and The Dogends.

The Poles.

Too Much Texas.

Haçienda staff room with Lyndsey.

With Brendon.

Gay Traitor bar.

Too Much Texas supporting New Order.

With Gordon MacKay of Too Much Texas.

Inspiral Carpets: (L to R) Clint, Tom, Martyn, Graham, Craig.

Noel.

Inspiral Carpets in the woods.

Inspiral Carpets being hard.

Inspiral Carpets postcard.

Soundcheck at GMEX 21.07.90.

Backstage in Ireland.

Like No.6 from *The Prisoner*. On stage, 1992.

Radio 1 event with Mark Goodyear, Amanda de Candenet, and Brinsley
Forde of Aswad and *The Double Deckers* fame.

One night on the endless solo acoustic tour.

The Lovers: (L to R) Steve Hanley, Kelly Wood,
Tom Hingley, Paul Hanley and Andrew Tarling.

her. We unpack and go upstairs to the pool where the crew are chilling. Anthony and Pete Donaldson are here. We buy a magazine called *Concept Barcelona*. They call up Michael Bell, an old Haçienda friend of Alison's, who is now living here. We go out for a meal in a vegetarian restaurant with the caterer Paul, Pete Donaldson and Binsey. The food is lovely. I find out the name of popular house music clubs for Mark and Noel to visit. Pete Donaldson and Paul the caterer go to the Phonogram concert where James are supporting Status Quo in front of 35,000 people in a warehouse. Martyn and Craig go to the after-show party hosted in a castle on a hill. We return to the hotel, shattered, and go to sleep.

26th May 1991: Barcelona, Spain

Get up, have breakfast in a street café near the hotel. I have spaghetti carbonara then go with Alison down to the beach in a cab, which takes forever. On the way we see the Olympic Village, which is under construction. What a mess! The beach is sad, but nice, there are lots of children playing. We walk back to the hotel from the Columbus column. We go up to the pool to see the entire crew chilling. Go for a Spanish meal. I enjoy traditional paella with mussels with plenty of red wine. Back to the hotel and sleep.

27th May 1991: Barcelona, Spain

We pack everything up in the room, and then go out to the posh shops. My throat is bad, and I am arguing with Alison about where to eat. Eventually we get Holly some Barbie accessories and the baby-to-be a romper suit. Back to the hotel, and get the concierge to bring the bags down. Karen and Alison leave for the airport, and the tour bus takes us to the concert. The crew bus driver who is driving Mark, Noel, Oz, Diane, Ed and Paul Fallon has been pissing the crew off by calling them 'druggy mongs'. The venue is big and I don't expect much audience. The road is busy and my throat is bad. Daniel Miller arrives and we have a meeting on the back lounge of the bus. Daniel suggests we call Brad Hunt at Elektra, because they hate the video for 'Please Be Cruel'. I learn from Graham that the French weren't happy with part of an interview I did in Paris with the magazine *Rock and Folk* because I sat on a scooter in the street for the photo, and the image didn't fit in with the way the band is being promoted, which is fair enough. The reporter also slagged Inspiral Carpets off in the piece. The concert is a bit shit, as my voice has packed up, especially with all the stage smoke, shaky. I dedicate 'Further Away' to Daniel. It's a real freak out which makes the concert. Sami from the record company seemed pleased. After the show, I feel ill and get on the bus for a nine-hour drive, drink Benilyn and sleep badly. Someone shits on the tour bus and fingers of blame get pointed.

### 28th May 1991: Madrid, Spain

Arrive at a Butlin's-style holiday camp, but the bus can't get down to the venue. Paul Fallon is annoyed. Eventually get there. I walk to catering and have bacon and eggs, and then go back on the bus for some sleep. A doctor comes and says that I have a cold and gives me some good medicine. I feel shit. Oz leaves to go and sort out the PA for the Happy Mondays gig at Leeds football stadium, Elland Road.

There is a kangaroo court to establish who shat on the bus. It turns out that it was the driver, as he says incriminatingly 'It's my bus, I can do whatever I want on it.' The venue is nice. I call Bruno at Mute France to discuss the *Rock and Folk* interview. He reassuringly says that the reporter was cynical and not to worry about it. Paul the caterer is acting like a mess officer in the army, organising everyone. The soundcheck is dicey, with my Lee Marvin 'Wandering

Star'-style voice. We have discussions in the production office about the girlfriend situation. Good! The concert is an absolute classic, real EMF stuff. Craig thinks I am one-hand clapping. After a lot of fuss we arrange to talk to Brad Hunt (our American manager) on the phone to discuss the video for the next single. The call was brisk, he was being the hard man, probably with good reason. We sit on the bus and Mansi cracks Erasure jokes. We watch *The Young Ones'* 'Video Nasty' and *Blackadder*. I can't sleep. Yark!

# 18

## The harder I try, it gets further away

My daughter Elsa was born in September 1991. She was born jaundiced and was kept in St Mary's hospital for an extra three days while she was treated with UV light. Within an hour of getting wife and baby home for the first time I had to fly 11,000 miles to Argentina to support Paul Simon with Inspirals. When the tour bus turned up, I brought Elsa out. I held her, small and wrapped in a bundle, and my desire, as would be any normal father's, was to show her off to friends and associates. At this point Noel made some crass, stupid, unnecessary and insulting comment, like: 'Why the fuck have you brought her out here?' It is a major regret to this day that I didn't deal with this situation more appropriately.

That was the second time we had visited Argentina. The first time, we arrived in Buenos Aires to perform on a popular television show and to do some interviews. We were driven around the incredible mixture of classic European cityscapes and mass industrial plots that made up the eclectic Argentinean infrastructure.

We attended a football game where Boca Juniors played competitors Internationale. Enormous inflatable sausages expanded out of the dugouts at opposite ends of the pitch. They looked like vertical versions of those gigantic anthropomorphic blow-up mascots that tyre and exhaust garages have wobbling around on their forecourts. The purpose of the sausages was to prevent opposing fans from throwing an assortment of darts, fireworks and bricks at the players as they arrived on the pitch. Once they had disgorged the players, the sausages wound back in like party balloons popped by a pin.

We collectively felt a deep sense of alienation in that home crowd. It would have been easy to tell, from how we spoke and the clothes we were wearing, that we weren't local, and Craig's signature ginger hair was something that seemed very rare in Argentina. On the way back, on one of the raised motorways, a car full of football fans tried to cut us up in our MPV. Martyn showed them the finger – not exactly an internationally recognised sign of peace and good will – and we were chased down the freeway and lost them on the off-ramp. A scary memory. It wasn't that long after the Falklands war, and I can remember the political signs hanging on many roads stating that the Malvinas were, and forever would be, Argentinean. It was only eight years since the pride and professionalism of the British Army took on a rag bag of sixteen-year-old boys from poor neighbourhoods, who often had no shoes or rifles.

Argentina was charming, with the utter kindness of the people who we met, and the makeshift roadside barbeques with piles of cooked meat and acrid wood smoke mixed with the smell of burnt fat. We performed on two television shows, one of which was shot in Buenos Aires. It was an incredibly popular Saturday-night show, watched by most of the population, a mixture of *Top of the Pops* and *The Good Old Days*. We realised it was a popular show the day after it was recorded, when we were walking round the wide boulevards of the capital city and were being recognised and greeted by everyone, from small children to old ladies.

The other show we filmed was recorded in Córdoba, the country's second city. We gave an interview and a performance. The two major channels on Argentinean TV were based in the same studio complex. We were sitting in the other channel's theatre where a very famous children's television show had just been filmed and a large audience of kids were gradually dispersing. A dozen ten-year-old children came and sat round us, inquisitive and aware of our oddness; they were very friendly. Perhaps they recognised us from the ubiquitous Saturday-night television broadcast, but they didn't understand a word of English. Anyhow, Clint sat there with them and, in a typical piece of Boonish black comedy, spoke to them in a gentle, pleasant, soft upbeat tone, but saying things that were incongruous, mainly about the Falklands War.

Graham went rooting through the theatre's costume department and found a bird's costume, with a full beak that extended out beyond the balaclava-like-hole for the eyes, and had thousands of multi-coloured sequins sewn into it and a mass of plumage, fashioned from genuine rare feathers. It also had wings that attached to the wearer's arms. This costume was designed to be worn by a small woman or child, and therefore didn't fit Graham's full build – he looked highly un-nerving when he slipped into it, and wore it on the chat show, all the while maintaining a wholly plausible matter-of-fact face. It must have been a strange vision for viewers to behold, an English indie musician dressed up as an iconic TV show character. The show was broadcast live and the staff had the responsibility of silencing Martyn as he was straining on a toilet; the sounds of his groans were being simultaneously aired on national television.

The bird costume of course went straight in the suitcase, and came back to the UK with us on our return. Graham still occasionally puts the costume on after concerts, and at significant family events, such as the important birthdays of his children. These worrying apparitions are often accompanied by him flapping his wings/arms in a futile attempt at flight, and a pathetic attempt at squawking, while maintaining afterwards a Superman/Clark Kent denial that it was actually him dressed as a bird. Lord knows what the children's TV show did once they found they had lost their costume.

Our return to Argentina was part of a dash around the world, doing sixteen flights in as many days. Our entourage included Binsey, Oz the soundman, Mark Coyle on monitors, Noel providing technical support, and a lady called Mel Corbould who worked in the international department of Mute. It was a strangled international journey where we crossed and re-crossed the Atlantic and Pacific oceans, starting off with a dash to Japan, then two concerts at either side of America in LA and New York, and then a flight down to South America, which stopped off in Brazil at Sao Paulo before heading on to Uruguay.

We arrived at Montevideo and stayed in a hotel nestled in one of the thousands of beachside tower blocks, which at first impression resembled the Spanish holiday apartments in Benidorm. The concert, in a small vibrant club, was a success. Uruguay had American-style two-pin electricity sockets, but 240 volt European-strength voltage. Oz unbelievably plugged in a series of American transformers for his Sony Walkman and each of them died with the sound of a tiny pop as the double-strength voltage fried them.

We flew on to Buenos Aires from Montevideo. When we arrived at the enormous, posh hotel, Mark, Oz and Noel were climbing the walls of their hotel room because they could almost smell the cocaine of the capital, but had no way of making a drug connection. Binsey was ordering £50 bottles of wine, which I guess the promoter was paying for, but those three crew hated wine.

I was invited out to a local club by the baseball-hat-wearing promoter. A lingerie show was taking place with

135

a collection of beautiful eighteen-year-old girls disporting themselves. It was only a week after I had become a first-time dad and I was feeling homesick and confused. I couldn't deal with the alienation of the scene, or the distance and separation of me from my wife and newborn child.

I got talking to the promoter, and he asked why the rest of the band and crew hadn't come out to the club. I told him that a few of the crew were trying to get some cocaine. He said that he had five grams in his hotel room, which he had obtained for the English band that were supporting Paul Simon on the second night of his River Plate festival gigs. I found out what room the promoter was staying in, and went back to the hotel.

I saw Mark and Noel and told them that the promoter had some coke, gave them his room number and went to bed. There was a certain degree of humour surrounding the fact that I, the squarest member of the entourage, had been the one to find them some fast drugs. I had once been interviewed on the telephone by an Australian journalist who thought he was talking to Chesney Hawkes, so I went along with it and pretended to be Chesney. I threw in the conversation the only two things I knew about my adopted persona; I said that my father had been in a Merseybeat band, had gone on to become a cocaine dealer and that's how my record deal was brokered. From that moment on our entourage, and especially Noel, would refer to coke as 'a bit of Chesney'.

In the breakfast room the next morning, the baseball-capped promoter approached me urgently, and in a hungover, worried voice said that he had drunkenly sold all five grams of the coke, and needed to get some back. I laughed and asked when he had sold the coke to them. He said it was six hours ago. I told him that it was pointless, our lot were from Manchester and would have snorted it all by now. Thus was born the legend of Noel Gallagher pouring cocaine onto his breakfast cornflakes.

When the other English band turned up the next day, they were highly nonplussed that the promoter's drug score for them had gone up strangers' and lessers' nostrils. The band wouldn't let us hang out with them, wouldn't let us ride round in their vehicles, and later totally failed to cop off with any of the eighteen-year-old lingerie models in the local club. We watched them support Paul Simon that night, and they were electric as they kicked into 'She Sells Sanctuary'.

It turned out that the guitarist's dad had worked with Melvin, Martyn Walsh's dad, as a brickie on sites in and around Manchester in the seventies and eighties. Small world. Despondent and drugless, the band had confided to us around the hotel pool that they were tired of wearing denim and leather, and would like to dress in the casual football-fan-inspired tracksuits and tops that we wore. Craig suggested that they wore whatever they wanted. In a subsequent interview in *Melody Maker*, the band wore casual attire in the photo shoot. We found out that they had been dropped by their record company some months later.

*IV*
*Revenge of the Goldfish*

# 19

## Monkey on my back

Noel was living with his girlfriend Louise Jones in a flat in the Bohemian atmosphere of India House, which was originally a big, textile-packing warehouse, but was converted into flats during the eighties. Despite this domestic arrangement, Graham and I started to suspect that a secret office romance was blossoming between Noel and Debbie, Clint's ex-girlfriend. Noel was very supportive of Debbie when she bravely took on the role of running our office, and protected us from the bollocks that Binsey was dropping.

A certain degree of flirting had been seen to go on between them, but after a few months it became an unspoken suspicion that they were soulmates. It was tricky, because we didn't know what Clint knew. Eventually the rumour spread out amongst our little community like ripples in a pool of water. I do wonder to what degree the emotional trauma of this time contributed to Noel's artistic genesis. It does make me question who or what Noel is referring to when I look at the lyrics for songs such as 'Don't Look Back in Anger'.

There is a line in Oasis' 'Married with Children' – 'Your music's shite, it keeps me up all night' – that was the cause of some speculation amongst the Inspiral Carpets. Some suggest that it's an ironic comment from Louise, and refers to his songwriting during this time, whereas others reckon that the lyric is a comment from Noel, directed at us…

# 20

## When I'm flying so high

Over the summer and autumn of 1991 we began the task of writing new material for the post-*Beast Inside* era. Debunked from the control freakery that typified our behaviour after the release of our first album, we decided to follow the advice of our mentor, Mute, by starting the process of finding a new producer, and attempting to record a couple of tracks for a stand-alone EP. Our desire to insist on who should produce future records had been effectively shattered by the spectacular misfiring of our second album, artistically and commercially, so we were up for any suggestions that Mute could offer.

Daniel Miller chose for us a Belgian producer called Pascal Gabriel, a former member of S'Express. Pascal was also a writer and member of Bomb the Bass who released records on Mute's subsidiary label, Rhythm King. He had recently produced a great single for the old punk band Wire called 'Eardrum Buzz', and their subsequent album, and had worked on a single remix for EMF's second album, *Stigma*. He was a safe pair of hands.

Pascal was bold, enthusiastic, punky and electro, with an enormous bank of out-board gear that he would bring into the studio. Possessing an Inspector Clouseau-esque accent, he was a powerful sounding board for the newly insecure Inspiral Carpets.

We moved into a rehearsal room above Colin Sinclair's office at The Boardwalk. Pascal would pull and tweeze the arrangements of our songs, as if they were a Stretch Armstrong toy, moulding them into a more poppy and commercial structure. I came up with two songs – one was called 'Smoking Her Clothes' and the second was a tune I had been writing for a couple of years. It began as I read the William Golding novel *Pincher Martin*; I took the basic idea and matched it with the recent events of the Gulf War to write 'Dragging Me Down'.

Pascal wrote the parts of the song as bars on a piece of paper, and suggested how we could improve the arrangement. He wanted to turn the song into a pop single, a trait missing in the overlong, perhaps self-indulgence of *The Beast Inside* with it's thirteen-minute epic 'Further Away'. This meant that the song could be built up throughout each section. Craig, always an encyclopaedia of good musical taste, suggested a Stetsasonic-style beat from 'Cross The Tracks' by Maceo & The Macks. It was cooking. Clint inserted fantastic filtered keys, Farfisa and back-feel to the track, and Graham copied the seven-note introduction guitar line at the beginning and big block chords that build up and down throughout like big bits of acoustic meccano. It was a million miles away from the New Age silences of *The Beast Inside* album. No complacency or taking the world's issues too seriously here.

We recorded 'Dragging Me Down' along with 'Smoking Her Clothes' and 'I Know I Am Losing You' in a studio in Wrexham called The Windings. It was easy reach for me in my silver, soft-top Mercedes 380SL, shooting down the M56 and turning left near the turn for Chester. Happy days indeed. Once we had completed the recording, I went down to a studio in London to re-record the vocals. The night before the vocal session, I stayed at Pascal's house in Islington and rode pillion on his dirty big motorbike into the studio the next morning. Once we had the main vocals nailed, Pascal handed me a big spliff and we moved on to the ad-libs for the middle and end sections. When I'd done, I took a taxi from the studio and the cabbie told me that his cousin, Richard West, had just joined the Shamen and was about to start recording the album *Boss Drum*, featuring 'Ebeneezer Goode'.

We debated with Mute as to which song would make the best A-side of our next single. I talked to Graham and asked which song he could imagine blasting out of a standard dirty, sweaty, indie disco, such as The Venue on Whitworth Street, where Dave Haslam cut his DJing teeth. We agreed that it had to be 'Dragging Me Down'. The B-side, 'I Know I Am Losing You', was mixed at Suite 16 in Rochdale, where I was the only band member present. The engineer Paul Rabiger and I decided to throw the kitchen sink at the song and it came out as a psychedelic classic. I think the B-side upset Pascal though; Paul didn't work on any more of the recorded productions we did with Pascal over the next two albums.

Just before the single came out, I was in John Brice's offices at Warner Chappell where I met a radio plugger called Jeff Chegwin. I reminded him of the lousy job he had done of promoting my brother's band's single 'Beauty Has Her Way' when he had tried to get them radio play, back in 1985. I played him 'Dragging Me Down' and left a copy with him. I am convinced that a mixture of guilt and love of our single made him go to Radio 1 and single-handedly ensure that the record got A-listed, even though he wasn't paid or officially working on the record.

We played a secret show, supporting Carter the Unstoppable Sex Machine, at Brixton Academy before the single release. We'd had a complicated relationship with Carter. In 1989, when Inspiral Carpets were breaking big all over the UK, Carter snapped at our heels by creating a pastiche of our Cool as Fuck T-shirts, as well as aping ones by James and the Mondays. Carter were having their third and last go at breaking into pop success and were throwing as much shit at the wall as possible to see what would stick, which made us wary of them initially. In 1990, after we signed a publishing deal with Chrysalis, Carter signed to Chrysalis Records and recorded a cover of 'This Is How It Feels', perhaps to repay their cheekiness.

John Fat Bastard, who was Carter's manager, was blowing our cover at the gig by walking around the foyer of Brixton Academy saying in a stage whisper, 'You won't believe who is playing a secret support tonight... Inspirals.' John was to Carter what Bez was to Happy Mondays, a kind of official ligger who went everywhere with the band.

Despite John spilling the beans, we came on stage playing our new single with the lights down and the curtain coming up to 4,500 people who had no idea who we were for the first fifteen seconds. With all those people, and half the producers from Radio 1, that was a smart move, and it paid off to be a hungry pop band making aggressive, catchy records again.

We were recording in Blackwing Studios in London when Daniel Miller arrived to tell us that 'Dragging Me Down' had charted at No. 12. 'This Is How It Feels', amongst the madness of Madchester, had peaked at No. 14, so this new chart high should have been greeted as significant. Daniel was really excited, but Graham and Clint were subdued in their response to the news.

# 21

## How d'you know I won't pray for you

We recorded our third album, *Revenge of the Goldfish*, at Blackwing Studios; the birthplace of many recordings by Fad Gadget, Depeche Mode, Yazoo and Erasure. It was housed in a deconsecrated church adjacent to Southwark Cathedral; its south aisle had been destroyed in the Blitz. Daniel Miller told us a creepy story about how a drum machine went mad, as if possessed by a demon spirit, in the middle of a Fad Gadget recording session, at 3:00am with only him and Frank Tovey in the control room. They discovered the machine was set to pattern 666! He might have been winding us up, but it was a powerful and scary place.

The insecurity created by the performance of *The Beast Inside* was now over and the gloves were off, as we were all back to competing to write singles for the band again. Clint was keen to get back in the songwriting/driving seat.

### Generations
Clint originated the words and music for 'Generations'. It celebrates the equidistant ages that separate his father's age from him, and Clint's from his first-born, Harley. 'You've got twenty-seven years on me'...

The song presents an underlying unspoken belief in the unrolling improvement of human affairs, underwritten by Clint quoting from Martin Luther King's 'I Have A Dream' speech: 'Free at last, free at last. Thank God Almighty we are free at last.' Many rave and house tunes of the time were borrowing, indeed actually sampling, from King's messages of love, acceptance and civil rights. Musically, the song's introduction owes more than a little to the Human League song 'The Sound of the Crowd'. Throughout, the choruses explode in long lines of singing, with no space or time for a singer's breath!

### Saviour

This is Martyn's song, a punk speed anthem with the hallmark Inspiral message of unrequited love. By the time this second song ended on the record, we felt we had set a very different mood to *The Beast Inside*; the crystal clear production, arrangement and songwriting setting a new agenda.

### Bitches Brew

Graham brought the seed of the song into the rehearsal room. It is quite usual that Graham's lyrics are esoteric, his songs can't be reduced to one unambiguous message, but 'Bitches Brew' does revisit many of the subjects touched on in Graham's 'She Comes In The Fall'. The title is a direct nod to the seminal 1970 jazz record by Miles Davis.

### Smoking Her Clothes

The title for this was a wordplay inspired by a Bob Dylan lyric in his song 'Memphis Blues Again'. The central image of smoke curling over a lover's repose and clothing was a powerful one to a committed chain-smoking singer at the time! 'She's wearing a cigarette and she's smoking her clothes.'

### Fire

'Fire' bears the hallmarks of a typical arrangement of mid-period Inspiral Carpets musical output. I started the song by writing riffs on a guitar to accompany some lyrics. It's a bit like The Doors, with a healthy crescendo towards the end, with Craig smacking ten bells of shit out of the snare, bass drum and hi-hat cymbals to underline the sheer pulsing sexual urgency of the song. Elizabethan plays often equate venereal disease with the many metaphysical and hellish fires of the soul and body.

Clint created the little call and response add-ons at the end of each chorus line, adding context to the relationship between two people experiencing the violence and passion of the fire's destructive qualities. The reference to 'We twist and turn in the whirlpool' relates to comments made by God's cop James Anderton, Chief Inspector of the Manchester Police, when he said that AIDS victims and anyone who was remotely counter-culture were culpable by their 'errant' behaviour and were to blame for their own fate because they were 'swirling in a cesspit of their own making'.

### Here Comes The Flood

I lifted part of this song from one that I wrote as a schoolboy with my Beatle-mad friend John Nesirky. I was once questioned backstage by Peter Gabriel's daughter as to why we had stolen a song title from him. This was true, albeit unwittingly. I did have a copy of his song of the same name.

Noel hated 'Here Comes The Flood' and on only its second live outing he expressed his antipathy towards it by mocking its 3/4 waltz time by making a wanking motion with one hand expressing a curve from the back to the front of his head earnestly in time to the song. We never played it again. I guess Noel must have had a change of heart later or forgot about his disdain of the timing when he composed 'Wonderwall' in triplets played over a 4/4 beat.

### Dragging Me Down

The William Golding novel *Pincher Martin* that was the inspiration for this song appears to tell the story of a sailor in the Second World War falling off a submarine and swimming to an island. However, at the end you discover that the hundreds of pages of description are allegorical, because the man actually drowned, his metal-weighted waders carrying him down to the bottom of the sea.

Musically this is a fifties doo-wop shuffle guitar riff; it has a similar feel to 'Summer Nights' from *Grease*. The guitars in the introduction sound like the beginning of 'Holidays in the Sun' by the Sex Pistols and the vocal lift in the chorus is taken from elements of the end of the Pistols' chorus in the song 'Submission': 'Down, down, dragging her down, Submission, I can't tell you what I've found.'

### A Little Disappeared

This song was written by Graham, and harks back to the band's initial singles. It feels like a song from the *Life* album. With its fairground Farfisa organ, grinding guitars, bass and vocals, it's a classic three-minute pop song.

### Two Worlds Collide

Clint put forward a track called 'Aphrodite's Children', which he had written on our first visit to Athens, contrasting the terrible poverty with the beautiful expensive ruins. Pascal suggested that we should take the chorus of one of Graham's songs, 'Two Worlds Collide', and weld it to the verse of Clint's Greek tragedy.

On the trip to Greece, while we were busy sleeping in the hotel, our Cypriot lighting director Loucas was revisiting Athens Zoo were he had spied a sad elderly eagle with its foot chained to a piece of stone. Struck by the cruelty to the animal, he returned at night, bunked over the wall and cut the eagle's foot loose with a hacksaw. Instead of flying away it just sat there not moving. Loucas tried to shoo it away to freedom but it was dead behind the eyes.

### Mystery

I wrote this rock song extolling the beauty of a woman at home on a guitar using big bar chords. Clint borrowed an enormous stylophone from Edgar Jones of the Liverpudlian band The Stairs. The stylophone had a picture of Rolf Harris on its packaging, and David Bowie had used it on 'Space Oddity'. Clint and Graham endlessly mimicked the end of the song: 'diddly diddly diddly diddly'. Noel hated it and we only ever played it live twice. Maybe he had a point, it isn't the most subtle of songs.

### Rain Song

Once again, we see Graham's habit of borrowing titles from pre-existing songs, in this case visiting the library of Led Zeppelin. The Zeppelin song itself was a conscious effort to write a ballad. At George Harrison's challenge and encouragement, they borrowed some chords from his 'Something'. Graham's song is melodic, spiritual and dreamy in a way that only songs germinated in his fertile imagination can be!

### Irresistible Force

Originated via Martyn and Clint, it's a bit different from the rest of the album in that it is influenced more by electronic musical genres and has a drum machine and sample loop on the track. It was an opportunity for Pascal to pour a bit of technology in. It is a powerful closing track, and lends a promise of future experimental directions that the band could go in, a kind of crossroads.

The recordings of the songs on *Revenge of the Goldfish* contain a lot of conscious dynamics, such as build-ups, crescendos and drop-down segments, with every song put through the producer's mangle by transcribing each and every bar of music. It was a cold approach, an exercise in making every song a pop-based three-minute number, with an easy-to-follow beginning, middle and end. It is understandable that we should want to avoid the self-indulgence of *The Beast Inside* arrangements, but a happier balance between the previous freedom and the benign dictatorship of Pascal's productions would need to be discovered in future recordings if arguments and tensions weren't to rise in the studio.

*Revenge of the Goldfish* was released on 5th October 1992 and reached its highest point of No. 17 in the charts.

# 22

# The temple which they built
# is an empty shell

Trouble in the Inspirals camp had been churning around for a number of years. Our manager Binsey was a complicated personality. He ran the Inspirals empire with a mixture of humour, cheek and bloody-mindedness. The relationship between the band and manager was funny, and one where Binsey's obesity became a running joke by the then-skinny band. He was a good foil to the quips of Clint, Graham and Craig. Binsey wore glasses, and that's why he got the nickname 'Binsey Smith'. He was only twenty-three when we turned over £1m as a business in the year 1990–1991.

Binsey was well connected in the mid-to late-eighties in Manchester's music scene, which revolved around the galaxy of musical planets and heavenly bodies who co-existed in the North West: Tony Wilson and Alan Wise, in the Factory part of space; Colin Sinclair and Sue Longford in The Boardwalk; Tony Michaelides and Alison Martin at Piccadilly Radio; and Phil Korbel at BBC Radio Manchester's *Meltdown* show. Binsey had been managing The Waltones and he'd secured them a small indie deal with a London-based label called Medium Cool. He initially added a lot to the Inspirals' success – he was hungry for kudos and money. We were a strong team, Clint always had a really good head for business and fairness in dealings, and Graham was good at sticking to ethical positions and building a consensus. Things ran fairly smoothly between the band and manager throughout the heady days of 1989 when they had secured my services as singer, organised the setting up of Cow Records as an independent label, got us a decent agent, sorted promotion staff and made sure we got paid.

Two areas became issues in the relationship between band and manager: one was glory, and the other was finance. By glory I mean the adulation that we, as musicians, were getting as a band, which Binsey wasn't really getting to the same degree. He sometimes found us tricky, and perhaps difficult and awkward to deal with. He used to call us 'the kids' when referring to us to industry professionals. As the members of the band had strong characters, maybe Binsey felt that he had to prove his management abilities beyond making us a continuing success. He could have had no complaints about how much he was getting paid. Our deal was that he received a sixth (16.66%) share of all the profit, as commission in return for exclusively managing Inspiral Carpets and no other artists – a good deal for him really when we were turning over £1m a year.

The rot set in around the time that the band went on a tour of Japan, just before the release of our second album. I argued that Binsey couldn't speak Japanese and should stay in Europe to oversee the setting up of the promotion of *The Beast Inside*. It was costing us thousands to fly everyone over there. Eventually, Binsey capitulated after a fair degree of debate and agreed to stay. However, the situation damaged our relationship and after that it always seemed to me that he was setting his eyes on new horizons, new club nights, new bands to promote and manage, which of course he wasn't then entitled to do.

Allied to Binsey's drifting enthusiasm and focus was a lack of concern where the budgetary control of our business was concerned. From early days we had Debbie running the Cow Records office, and we appointed Brenda Clegg as our bookkeeper. Despite constant moaning by the band, the tax affairs always seemed to be concluded late and in an unsatisfactory and over-expensive manner. One of the first real lessons we learned as a band was to manage our expectations. We had sold 300,000 copies of our debut album by the autumn of 1990, and we expected to be receiving a hefty record royalty, but when it arrived, the sum was a disappointing £3,500. We had forgotten that Mute had paid us a £60,000 record company advance upon signing; therefore, there wasn't any more money due at that point. We probably learned more about the music business in that moment than over our entire band career.

After a year, we sacked our accountant because the accounts were consistently late, and the service unsatisfactory. We heard that New Order said that the accountant had wrongly advised that profits generated by the Haçienda wouldn't be subject to tax! We took our tax affairs to the London Irish firm of OJK. Our problems with them would happen a few years later.

A worrying part of Binsey's behaviour was his spending habits. In 1991, installed in our plush offices in New Mount Street, Shudehill, Binsey would go on spending sprees with one of our six company credit cards. At a meeting we called after the disappointing record royalty, we went through how much money each company director had run up on their respective cards. I had bought a guitar tuner for £60, and no one else had spent anything, apart from Binsey who had run up some £6000 on turntables, DIY items from B&Q, and expensive electrical items. The Cow office was becoming like the set from *Only Fools and Horses* – there were ten TV sets from the dance floor of the Haçienda, which Binsey had bought cheaply in order to sell on at a profit. It also came to light that he had bought four pairs of Technics DJ decks at £200 a pop, and that one set had gone missing. I said he had a week to find the missing deck, or pay for it. I also insisted that Binsey paid the band back all the money that he owed to the business.

It was usual for Inspiral Carpets to keep some of our touring crew on retainers when we weren't touring, paying a regular wage of £70 per week in order that we were guaranteed their services for the thirty or so days a year that we were playing concerts. Binsey used some of the members of crew that we had on retainers at his weekly dance club event, Space, at the newly owned Manchester Academy venue. He was offsetting some of the costs of his nights by using Inspiral Carpets' crew members, so the band was paying the wages which Binsey was then using to pay for work they were doing for him, work that we weren't getting paid for.

Over 1991 and 1992, Binsey began to manage more and more artists, despite the fact that he wasn't actually allowed to. He took on the band Medalark 11, who were made up from the ashes of the great Manchester band The Bodines. He also took on A Certain Ratio, the ex-Factory band, who were re-releasing their material on CD through Creation records. He was also managing a few clubs and remix DJs.

As time went by, all the various projects that Binsey was involved in were causing the members of Inspiral Carpets unease. Noel, Debbie and Brenda were ready informants about the number of drum kits that were arriving for Medalark 11, but which had been secured under sponsorship deals under our name. Brenda was very outspoken and began a root-and-branch investigation through all the things that were going wrong in our office and in our business.

During the 1991 New Year's Eve celebrations I was at a party at the Haçienda and Binsey had confided in me that he believed that the following year would bring mass indifference to the quickly cooling Manchester scene, and that things would be hard for Inspiral Carpets. I had to think on my feet; I realised that Binsey's admission meant that he had lost faith in us, and that managing us might now be difficult, so he was thinking about moving on. I saw my arse, because this meant that we might have to pay Binsey up to £80,000 compensation in return for him surrendering his sixth of the shares in the limited company, and that he might be telling me this because he wanted an easy way out. I kept quiet about what he had said as it wasn't the right time to act.

Financial and managerial problems came to a head in a variety of ways. Firstly, we had loads of people turning up at the Cow office who were nothing to do with the band or its affairs. They were somehow involved in the myriad of activities that Binsey was now involved with, but were nothing to do with us. These strangers would turn up and unceremoniously have the cheek to ask us who we were. It must have been a smaller, cheaper version of the chaos that ensued at The Beatles Apple Headquarters in the late sixties after Brian Epstein had died, and a thousand cranks, wannabees and fleecers were bleeding the soon-to-be-not-so Fab Four dry, with their artistic non-starters and get-rich-quick schemes. Secondly, any concept of budgetary control or accountability had gone. Binsey had set up a tab at the in-house café in New Mount Street and we were routinely running up £50 bills a week for the staff who we were paying wages to. We told him that this had to stop: it was our money that they were spending.

Around this time Binsey employed a company run by Tim, an ex-policeman, to try to put a stop to the fairly major bootlegging taking place outside our live shows. Such a procedure is always a moral dilemma, especially as selling bootleg T-shirts had been my first job in the music industry way back in the early eighties in Oxford. Also, as performers we all lived cheek by jowl, visiting the same clubs, bars and gigs as the ticket touts, dealers and bootleggers. Craig got threatened by a bootlegger days after Tim had impounded a lot of bogus gear outside our Manchester gig. A few days later, the intercom on the Cow office door buzzed and in came a young gentleman who punched Binsey, threatened him and left. A frustrating situation arose when we had paid Tim's company thousands of pounds to impound a load of bootleg gear, and it mysteriously disappeared again soon afterwards, probably to be resold.

As a band, we were generally never that keen on prosecuting bootleggers, because of our belief that if you are successful, you have to be prepared to let others make money from you further down the line. In a strange way, bootlegging was a compliment and a form of acceptance, Manchester nodding back to you that you had arrived. Frequently the designs of the bootlegged shirts were actually better than our official ones and we borrowed ideas from them. Like a lot of the things that happened back in those Madchester days; business-culture, records and fashion were all part of one big conversation that was going on between disparate groups, even if some of the individuals involved were people you really wouldn't want to bring home to meet your mum and dad. The place was richer for it.

The band's finances became a matter of concern as, despite turning over hundreds of thousands of pounds, we always seemed to be skint. Accounts would be filed late, we would incur fines or, worse, threats from the Tax Office to take us to court or strike off our limited company.

One night Graham, Clint and I called in the office and, on Brenda's instruction, looked through some books of invoices of goods and services that our company had paid for. What we found was horrifying: a lot of invoices that we'd paid were either for Binsey's personal use or were for his other businesses. These items were for a couple of thousand pounds – not a few pennies here and a few dimes there. We had paid for the sound-proofing for A Certain Ratio's rehearsal room, plus banners and decals for Binsey's Space club night, where the likes of Jon Dasilva were DJing. There was an embarrassing moment when we asked Jon Dasilva to do a remix of 'Dragging Me Down' as an extra track for the single release. When we asked him who his manager was, he looked blank and then said, 'It's Binsey – didn't you know?'

This conflict of interest in our affairs annoyed Mute – they weren't pleased that Binsey was representing other people when he should have been looking after us to earn his sixth share. On one occasion, Mute were furious when promotional posters for one of our singles were obliterated by posters for one of Binsey's club nights. When Mute complained, Binsey just suggested that if they paid the poster folk some more money, they would put our posters back up over his.

One day a debt collector came looking for Binsey in relation to an unpaid bill from a company that arranged visas for Americans who wanted to enter the UK to work. Earlier, Ken, an employee of Mute America, had asked Binsey if he could sort out the travel documents for him to come over from the States to work in the UK. Binsey, being keen to help anyone who might be able to assist with any of his roster of artists and DJs stateside, offered to take care of it and even pay the £600 for the service. A year later, he used one of our cheques to pay for it. He had previously created an invoice-checking system on the office computer, which he then tried to destroy, but Brenda managed to recover it. We were reaching the point at which we had the proof that he was out of his depth and not acting in our best interest at all. It was time to go our different ways.

By now, our wives and girlfriends were becoming increasingly tired of us bitching about the problems with management and business, and they told us to stop moaning and actually do something about it. On 16<sup>th</sup> September we filmed 'Generations' on *Top of the Pops*. The following day, we visited our lawyer, Tony English, at Russell's in London, and, in Binsey's absence, drew up a legal document which gave him 30 days notice that we were dispensing with his services. That night we drove back up to Manchester and met at Graham's house in New Moston. We watched our *Top of the Pops* performance, our wives and partners still not believing that we were going to give Binsey the boot. We had hired a Luton van with a tail lift and, with the help of Noel, his brother Liam and Paul McArthur, we stripped everything out of the office and transported it to Alison's clothes factory on Ancoats Street. We even hoovered the floors and took all the blu-tack off the walls. Ironically, that night was the inaugural meeting and meal of the International Managers' Federation, where Binsey was enjoying himself for the last time on us!

The next day we all went back into the office and awaited Binsey's arrival. He turned up and, seeing the office empty, he smiled nervously, perhaps thinking for a nanosecond that the whole thing was some kind of wind-up. We handed him the severance letter from our lawyer, then asked him for our company mobile phone back. Binsey left, and that was the last time I ever saw him.

The rest of that morning we called up Mute, Chrysalis and all of our suppliers and business contacts, and told them not to discuss our business dealings with Binsey. Whenever the phone rang, Martyn, assuming that the caller was hoping to speak to Binsey, would answer it by making donkey noises into the mouthpiece. Brenda called the police and they interviewed Binsey in the station about allegations of possible fraud, the misrepresentation of cheques for goods that he had used, services the company hadn't used, and faking signatures. It wasn't a very sophisticated steal really.

The following week, Binsey appointed a lawyer, Steven Lee, who also worked for The Charlatans. Before Steven turned up, I said to the rest of the band that Binsey would probably have briefed him that we were behaving like spoilt children, and that we had behaved in an unacceptable way, so I suggested that we should come across as reasonable as possible. When Steven walked in, we all shook his hand and smiled to show we had no doubts or dissension. We offered him a cup of tea and asked him what tall stories our ex-manager had told him, and what Binsey wanted.

As prophesied, Steven said that Binsey was prepared to sue for damages and defamation, but that he would be prepared to hand his sixth share in the company back to us for a princely sum of £80,000. We said that if Binsey wanted to pursue that course of action, we would have no option but to involve the police. Steven's confidence seemed to crumble during the meeting. As he left, we told him that Binsey had a bad track record of not paying for professional services rendered.

I am still sad that we parted company with Binsey Smith this way, and there is little doubt in my head that, without Binsey's involvement, we would not have become the success that we fleetingly were. It was him who asked me to audition for the band in the first place. He went in too deep, beyond what he could handle, and he flew too near the sun and got his wings burned. To be fair on him, we were probably an absolute nightmare at times, but dealing with us is what he was so well paid for.

Once the dust had settled, we moved our gear back into New Mount Street and prepared for the imminent release of our third album.

# 23

## Just a nail I could hammer home

16th September 1992, the day we decided to part company with Binsey Smith, was an infamous day in British history. It became known as Black Wednesday, the day when the pound was forced out of the Exchange Rate Mechanism, the financial yoke created by the John Major Government designed to try to strengthen sterling in order that it might join the Euro when it was actually created. That same day we were sitting in a dressing room in Elstree studios with EMF, waiting to film a performance for *Top of the Pops*. EMF's bass player Zac Foley was using a Stanley knife to cut the ties off the curtains and claimed to be looking for a German 'to stab' because of the day's events and the rise in interest rates.

Earlier, Clint and I had shared a lift with Manic Street Preachers. Our relationship with the Manics was a complex one. There had been a war of words between them and Inspirals, with Nicky Wire trouncing our singles in the review sections of the *NME*. A few years later we attended the *NME* Brat Awards show and Clint had a humorous exchange with James Dean Bradfield where he said that, if I passed away, James would have to replace me as Inspiral Carpets' singer. James said, jokingly, to me, 'For Christ's sake, don't die, will you, Tom!' To be honest, they are really nice people and the spats between us and them were probably based on mutual respect and possibly envy on our behalf, of their success and talent.

With Binsey gone, we started the search for a new

manager. We talked to Martine McDonagh who managed James, but she was too busy with their success. Simon Napier-Bell, ex-Manager of The Yardbirds and Wham!, came out of the woodwork and attended our London concert at Brixton Academy on the *Revenge of the Goldfish* tour. News spread throughout the place within hours of him coming to the show, but I felt that it was just a piece of self-promotion on his behalf and that what we needed was someone more contemporary, a safe pair of hands. I didn't feel he was the man for the job. We then began discussions with Chris Morrison at CMO. Chris had managed Thin Lizzy throughout their career, The Jesus and Mary Chain, Elastica and, most significantly for us, Blur.

We had a meeting with Chris in his plush London office which seemed to be stuffed full of beautiful girls. We had what seemed to be a very good, funny chat with him, and he seemed to be quite keen to know more. He agreed to meet Daniel from Mute, but after that he declined the offer to manage us. Perhaps Daniel enlightened Chris to what Mute had in mind for Inspiral Carpets? Who knows.

It was a brave new world managing ourselves, and there was only us to blame if we couldn't pay our bills, or if recordings went wrong or albums didn't get promoted properly. We used a tour manager called Phil for a nightmare UK tour. Phil was useless. He would sit in the pub getting pissed, then roll up to the gig at seven o'clock and ask why the soundcheck hadn't been completed. We would find conflicting invoices for his expenses – car hire in Northern Ireland and a pizza restaurant bill from Cardiff on the same day, at the same hour. Rumour had it that he had once tour-managed Morrissey at an Italian Festival and had left £11,000 worth of currency in a pillowcase in his hotel room, and had only realised after boarding a plane.

After the UK tour, Phil tour-managed us on a quick hop

round the world with two gigs on either coast of America. On the flight back from the states we got upgraded to first class because Phil had good contacts with British Airways. Noel had been so snotty during the trip that Phil refused to upgrade him, so he sat alone in economy. One band member referred to him having his 'first class bottom lip out' as he walked dejectedly to the back of the plane.

Once we had got through customs and picked up all our gear from the baggage depot, we were driven in a van back to The Boardwalk, where we rehearsed. Straight off a transatlantic flight, and there we were, all five of us loading our gear up five flights of rickety stairs. Craig was moaning, so I said to him, 'Have you got fifty quid in your pocket to pay someone to load this gear in for us?' to which he said 'No.' 'Well shut the fuck up then. It's bad enough having to do it without you moaning about it as well.' I was all heart.

We decided to employ a friend of Alison's to be the tour manager for the European tour. Jane Roberts had been a bass roadie, and later girlfriend, of New Order's Peter Hook. Jane was a fantastic tour manager and skilled at running a bus with ten men on it.

We had a gig at a venue called Chez Paulette in Barine in France, near Nancy, which is a legendary venue and restaurant. We travelled overnight and, within minutes of arriving, Craig threw up the contents of his stomach down a storm drain in the road. Noel and Mark said that we should throw the gig and go home, but we told them to get real. At about 4:00pm we were ravenous, and the venue fed us loads of seafood. Poor Craig. A few of the band and crew didn't like what was served up and, to add insult to injury, two film crews from local television channels started filming us eating the gruel.

Jon Leshay came to visit us from the States, as did Bruno from Mute France. We gave Jon an Ecstasy tablet and he started getting loved up. Bruno fed us brandy and champagne and played us a pre-release copy of 'I Feel You' by Depeche Mode, which was fantastic. At the end of the night, the coach driver reversed the tour bus up the mile-long narrow track. Streams of cars full of people who attended the show kept overtaking the bus and forced us to stop our reversing.

We were now roaring drunk thanks to Bruno. Brandy and champagne is what the troops used to be given to encourage them to go over the top in the trenches in the First World War, not too far from where we were. Craig got out and put his hand out in a flat gesture to stop the traffic, but the French driver of the car in front of the long queue was, unfortunately, equally drunk, so he drove at Craig at full speed. In one graceful movement, Craig ran up over the top of the car and pulled the spoiler off the back windshield. In quick response, the occupants of the other cars went mad and started being really aggressive. They got out of their cars and chased him around as if we were all in a speeded-up filmed skit from Benny Hill or a silent film of the Keystone Kops. I jumped down from our bus and, as a distracting strategy, ran up and kicked the front door of the offending car. Jane shouted over and over again at the top of her voice: 'Get back on the bus! Get back on the bus.' Meanwhile, the Keystone Kops chased Craig round our tour bus until he climbed in the back door and locked it shut. As I got back on, Jane bravely stepped off and spoke to the mob before things escalated and the tour bus got stoned or set on fire by an angry French mob!

Jane persuaded the occupants of the cars to drive down to the end of the lane where we would agree to pay for the damage that Craig and I had done to their car. They drove off and Jane got back on the bus and we began reversing again, until we got to the end of the lane, where the driver turned the tour bus around and we drove off at top speed into the night. Some miles down the road, we discovered the kicked-in car upside down in a ditch. We stopped the tour bus and tried to help the occupants, but they responded by holding up their Gallic fists, so we got back on the bus and drove on to the next city. Suddenly sober.

Our driver was called Yorky. He used to run red lights, and, when we asked him why he kept doing this, he said, 'I will go for the reds first and pot the other colours later.' He once bought a cooked chicken in France, and didn't refrigerate it, yet was still pulling bits off it four days later in Germany. On one occasion Craig asked Yorky what the bright lights were that we were speeding towards. Yorky answered placidly, 'It's the border.' Suddenly, with thirty seconds' notice, all the recreationals on the tour were hidden away before the border guards and their dogs came on. Craig stashed some resin in an enormous can of Nestlé coffee granules. When he came to retrieve it, he found another seven blocks also hidden within.

On the last day of the tour, Noel and Mark vandalised the back of the bus by ripping a seat cover up and tagging the underside of the seat with crude drawings concerning the band, tour manager and bus driver. Graham took the decision that we wouldn't tell Jane as it would upset her, which led to a big argument, as we would have to admit to the damage and pay for it anyway. I think we all knew that the days of Noel and Mark working for us were over, and to be fair, the feeling was mutual.

Some weeks later, when we were back in Manchester, we got together with Noel and told him that we couldn't afford to employ him anymore. Noel wasn't at all bothered. He had started playing in a band with his brother.

# 24

## I've found a new girl,
## she's all I wanted for

Upon returning from the tour of the United States with his 'first class bottom lip out', Noel had found out that his younger brother Liam had formed a band called The Rain, along with his friends Paul Arthurs (Bonehead), Paul McGuigan and Tony McCarroll. Noel watched them play and decided they were rubbish. He took over their songwriting, then managed and moulded them into possibly the most successful band of the last thirty years.

Reputedly, Noel got the name of the band from a gig that Inspiral Carpets did on *The Beast Inside* tour at the Swindon Oasis Centre. Very early on in Oasis' career, it became clear that this musical departure was going to become more important to Noel than working for Inspiral Carpets. We had to get a replacement drum roadie for a Manchester Academy show in 1992 because Noel's new band were playing a show out of town on the same night. For a short time we rehearsed next to Oasis, and at the beginning I only remember them being able to play three songs: an obscure house tune which featured the line 'I wanted you to know'; 'One' by U2; and I seem to remember them clawing their way through a version of the Inspiral Carpets' 'Saturn 5' a year before it had even been released.

Their rehearsal room was in the cellar of The Boardwalk, where the walls were covered in a myriad of iconic images, including a Union Jack, pictures of The Who and The

Beatles. Even back then they had their own very big vibe of greatness emanating from that cinder-block walled space, homage to thirty years of pop and popular music culture, and they used to play loud. I had a bit of a spat with Noel over the summer of 1993 when I came back from a summer holiday and found that Clint had lent Oasis our PA and speakers. I went to their rehearsal room to get it back, and found that most of the Piezo tweeters in the Peavey speakers were blown out from the whole thing being played through way too loudly.

I attended two early Oasis gigs; the first was their second gig at The Boardwalk in January 1992, and then supporting Peter Hook's side project, Revenge, at Middleton Hippodrome in April. I went to The Boardwalk gig out of a sense of solidarity to Noel to show that I was supportive of my old rival's new band. The Middleton gig I attended to avoid watching the Freddie Mercury Memorial concert that was on BBC1 that night.

To be honest, although I was looking at the future of rock and roll, haircuts, fashion and lads popular culture, I just didn't get it. I didn't understand what their revolution was, nor what it represented. This was the culmination of that Stone Roses gig at the International 2, where Graham had met Noel. Here was the summation of some 200 sweaty gigs where Noel had stood at the side of the Inspirals stage, watching us winding up an audience like a watch spring. Absorbing the vibes, the camaraderie, the songwriting dynamic, the humour, the gang mentality, the pulling yourself up by your boot straps, the throwing-as-much-shit-at-the-wall-and-seeing-how-much-would-stick approach, and not worrying too much about being controversial and upsetting folk.

Noel approached me after The Boardwalk gig, surprised and pleased that I had come, as there weren't any other members of Inspirals present. He told me that an Oasis demo had somehow made its way to Johnny Marr, and then on to his manager, Marcus Russell, at the management company Ignition. He seemed to think that Marr might produce some songs for Oasis, and that a record deal was not far off. I was genuinely pleased for him.

In the autumn of 1992, local journalist Penny Anderson devoted her Friday pop page in *The Word* to Oasis. There was a picture, by local Madchester photographer Pete Walsh, where the band was framed looking down from a viaduct in Castlefield. Alison looked at it and said, 'They are going to be fucking massive!' I had an underlying feeling that she was correct, knowing what a big soul Noel had, and a mouth that was ever so slightly bigger still.

The band that rehearsed alongside Oasis at The Boardwalk was Medalark 11. They were signed to Creation Records and for two years they were rehearsing cheek by jowl with Oasis. The Oasis lads mocked Medalark 11's support of Manchester United by scrawling the traditional Manchester City supporters sick insult of 'Munich '58' in biro on their rehearsal room door. I presume that Creation Records boss Alan McGee must have been floating around at this time and it would have been difficult for such big and territorial characters as Oasis to avoid contact with any record company executive who might have been visiting The Boardwalk rehearsal space around 1991–1993. The rock and roll myth making that says Alan McGee 'spotted' Oasis onstage at a gig at King Tut's Wah Wah Hut in Glasgow on 31ˢᵗ May 1993 was a sign of things to come.

Our ex-manager, Binsey, had gone on to manage Medalark 11 towards the end of his stint with us and he tried to muscle in on managing Oasis, but Noel, way too smart from hanging around with us, told him to forget it. Once Oasis had signed to Creation and released their first single 'Shaker Maker', they appeared on an edition of the TV show *The Word* and played 'Supersonic'. By the end of the performance, the whole nation had fallen in love with them.

At the Manchester music In The City event in the autumn of 1994, I was on the judging panel for new bands, which was a central part of the event at that time. After we had given the prize to the winners, I got talking to a fan who said that he had just got a lift up the M6 from London to Manchester with Mani, bass player from The Stone Roses, and he had played the chap their new, and as yet unreleased album, *The Second Coming*. The lad held his hand up, said 'Oasis' and made a blowing sound, as if suggesting that the arrival of the Roses' second album would have the affect of knocking Oasis and their success off trajectory. I said to him that he was wrong, that Oasis would be much bigger than The Stone Roses, that the Roses were amazing, but that they had squandered their primary, pole position, creatively and artistically, by standing still for too long.

Noel could have learned what he needed working for The Stone Roses, but their egos would have been too big to accommodate him, even in 1990 when he was acting out the general role of everyone's best mate and roadie for us. He couldn't have learned at the hands of Happy Mondays because hard drugs and bickering would have hampered his musical education. Noel was very clever to attach himself, limpet-like, to the bottom of the Inspiral Carpets' Noah's Ark. His musicality, wit and intelligence were his own, but he borrowed inspiration from The Stone Roses; fun, controversy and drug iconography from the Happy Mondays; and a sense of brotherhood, fraternity and sheer bloody-minded hard work from Inspiral Carpets. As well as humour and catchphrases, of course.

I kept myself in a happy state of denial in regards to Oasis and their irreversible climb up into the heights of pop culture for all time. It was only in the summer of 1994, when on tour in the former Eastern Bloc states of the Czech Republic and Slovenia with Moby, that Craig forcibly played me *Definitely Maybe* on the tour bus' stereo. He made it clear to me that Oasis were really something special and that I should stop acting stupidly about it. He was 100% right. It was wonderful music, and we should be rightly proud of our compatriot taking the torch further than we ever could. In pop music terms, we had taken a walk in the park, whilst Noel had gone to the moon and dragged everyone else in the world there, screaming for him.

There is a photograph of Inspiral Carpets playing a concert at the now sadly defunct Newport venue called TJ's, and at the front of the audience are two fans wearing Oasis T-shirts. This shot would have been taken somewhere between the autumn of 1992 and the summer of 1994, the narrow band of time when the two bands' touring lives co-existed.

In the autumn of 1993 Inspiral Carpets and Oasis were both booked in to do a Radio 1 gig at a music event called Sound City in Glasgow, at a venue called the Tramshed. It was a little odd sitting backstage with the total role reversal – they were the big stars, and no longer employees. Bonehead was projecting his pop star profile by ordering gin and tonics and affecting stand-offishness. I suppose both sets of people were readjusting to the new lay of the land.

Inspiral Carpets played Glastonbury Festival in 1994. We played on the second stage, which was called the *NME* stage at that time. Liam was now on a year-long tirade to rubbish all things Inspirals in order to push Oasis and to separate themselves from his and Noel's previous association with us. Oasis had played earlier on in the day and Liam was saying that it was an outrage that a band like Inspiral Carpets were higher on the bill than them. We never retaliated to such provocation, partly because we realised why Liam was saying these negative things, and also because I did see the light that day when Oasis played a fantastic set in front of one of the best Glastonbury audiences ever – Noel's guitar on fire, as the feedback was looped through an old Echoplex tape echo at the end of 'I Am the Walrus'.

Although we were booked to play on the Saturday, we hired a tour bus to be on site for the Saturday and Sunday, which meant that we could hang out and watch other bands, and didn't need to go ten annoying miles to stay in a decent and expensive hotel. This meant that on the Saturday night, Noel and Mark Coyle camped out and smoked draw on our bus, rather than having to get back to their distant and inconvenient hotel. It was really strange having them back on an Inspirals tour bus, when they had effectively bullied and trashed their way round the last one we had been on with them in Europe in 1992. However, it was a nice kind of dreamy déjà-vu to see them on the way to the stardom that they had discussed on the American tour bus just three years before. It was strange because, in one way everything had changed forever, and in another way something was exactly the same – you would need to be a Hindu scholar to process that combination of opposites held in place at the same moment.

On the Sunday, Noel, the new cock of the walk, was walking down the end of the row of tour buses whilst we were standing in front of ours. He was of course being pursued by a gaggle of music photographers. We waited until he reached us, and shook hands with him out of friendliness and a natural sense of sociability. Six months later, the photographs were reproduced in the music press as an example of how the hopelessly outmoded and out-gunned Inspiral Carpets were trying to seek favour by going out of their way to exploit Oasis' premiership by affecting association with them. The press can be so sad in its myth making.

By auditioning Noel on the night of the Lockerbie bombing, 21$^{st}$ December 1988, then choosing not to have him as the singer but to employ him as a roadie and guru, Clint, Craig, Martyn and Graham set Noel Gallagher on the path towards supernova stardom. The Inspirals allowed Noel complete unfettered access to a whole array of business meetings with record companies, publishers, producers, video directors, agents, promoters, accountants and lawyers. He had invaluable media training whilst working for Inspirals; he would sometimes sit in for a tired band member on promotional shots on tour in a foreign country. Somewhere in Europe and the United States there will be a load of photos of Noel standing in for me or Clint.

Noel met many influential people whilst involved with Inspirals: Paul Weller, who he first met at a rehearsal room in London when we were rehearsing to be on a *South Bank Show* end-of-year round up programme at the end of 1991; The Real People, who toured as support to Inspiral Carpets in 1991 and who produced Oasis' first single 'Shaker Maker'; Mark Coyle, our monitor engineer who went on to co-produce their debut album *Definitely Maybe*; Simon Moran, the promoter; Alan McGee; Red Alert, the promotions company; Daniel Miller and hundreds of other bread-and-butter music industry contacts.

Oasis knew how to control the news agenda, never more so than with the war with Blur. Up until the hiatus of their third album, Oasis were bigger than North Sea Oil, the Royal Family and *EastEnders* all put together. One of the things that always amused me during the single race between Oasis and Blur was something Noel had said way back when we were in the original Cow office. Noel always liked to wind us up by saying how he had seen a new band in town that were better than us. One day he said he'd seen a really good band playing the previous night at the university, and that the singer was climbing all over the stage and throwing himself all over the band's drum kit. The band's name? Blur.

*V*
*Devil Hopping*

# 25

## Where has that smile on your face gone?

The band saw the cutting away of Noel as a kind of emotional and spiritual liberation. Inspired by sacking him, Graham wrote the chord structure and I penned the lyrics to a song called 'How It Should Be', taking the notion from a Japanese saying which translates as 'tall nails get hammered down'. The others felt liberated enough to finally reveal to me that Noel had auditioned to sing in the band before I was taken on, a cardinal secret kept from me up until that point.

We recorded 'How It Should Be' along with two other songs at a recording session at FON studios in Sheffield. Still on the rebound from the experience of the *Revenge of the Goldfish* sessions, the idea was to explore the fresher, less technology-led sessions and try to find a more 'authentic' sound before commencing the recording of our fourth studio album – the fourth of the five that we had committed to when we signed the record deal with Mute back in the winter of 1989.

Mute were committed to funding Inspiral Carpets to the tune of £60,000 a year in advance as wages and on top of that, funding all the recording, manufacturing, advertising, promotion, including videos, and then paying us a 50% share of the profit that was left, but they couldn't go on honouring the deal unless they were making a healthy profit. We had seen a progressive decline in sales with each of our albums, so it was now make-or-break time.

When Clint played 'Saturn 5' for the first time in our

rehearsal room, I got a tingle down my spine. I knew that the song was a classic single from the first listen. When we played the song to Daniel Miller, he couldn't hear that it was a hit. If Daniel couldn't hear the potential in a song like 'Saturn 5', then we were finished on his label.

# 26

## No one ever said it was gonna be easy

We set up camp at Parr Street Studios in Liverpool to begin work on our fourth album proper with Pascal Gabriel at the production helm again. The name of the album, *Devil Hopping*, was coined by Clint as a jokey response to the way that Pascal pronounced the word 'developing' when describing the evolution of a song.

Twelve songs eventually made it on to what was to be the final Inspiral Carpets album, though of course we didn't know that at the time.

*I Want You*
Lyrically, this song seems to be about fucking, unrequited love and feelings of possession – quite standard fare for a song written by Martyn. We started playing it as a four-piece when Martyn initially brought it in as an idea because Clint couldn't make the writing session that particular day. I think Clint's absence at that session steered the development in a radical, punky-fuelled direction. The song doesn't feature much of the Farfisa on the verses. The guitar descends into Dead Kennedy-style plunges in the introduction and breaks, and the drum pattern is a three-minute, repetitive-strain-injury-inducing drum solo, wonderfully played by Craig.

I became obsessed with Ian Astbury's singing after seeing him sing with The Cult in Argentina. I wanted my voice to recreate the metallic hardness of Astbury's tone, which I tried on this track. Melodically, I borrowed from the approach that Gerry Rafferty uses in the Stealers Wheel song 'Stuck in the Middle With You', where the melody line keeps on returning to a single drone note, irrespective of what the rest of the tune is doing, to underline the idea that the song is about being in a rut or on a one-dimensional journey to a specified destiny.

## Party In The Sky

This is a bit of a mainstream rock song that I wrote in the key of A; it sounds a little like INXS. The biblical references to St Peter founding the church of Christ on a rock, and not sand, underline the fracture that was going on in my marriage at the time. I had married Alison at the age of twenty-six, and I was too young, perhaps trying unconsciously to prove to my six older siblings that I was mature.

## Plutoman

Clint wrote this luscious descriptive song about a magic dreamer. 'Even out here where he sits drowning in isolation, he's stacking his bricks high and slowly walling out the world.' It is very psychedelic in its approach.

## Uniform

I remember us slogging through this song when rehearsing on the top floor of The Boardwalk sometime in 1991. It was an old favourite of Daniel Miller and had been kicking around as a song from the writing of the third album, but somehow we just didn't seem to be able to get the song to sound right, and we gave up on it. Once we got stuck into the songwriting cycle for *Devil Hopping*, Daniel begged us to have another go at it.

The song is a sentimental appeal to soldiers and the sacrifice they make. I think Clint was reacting to the experience of spending time with his young American wife's family, and drawing from their life views. The song and the video are reminiscent of the first Gulf War, and the fighter pilots who got shot down and then terrorised by Saddam Hussein. We filmed the video in New York near the war memorials in Battery Park and in a suburb of Brooklyn where we set up a sixties montage of a family waving their son away into the army. Craig returned to the UK to support his girlfriend Rose as her mother had fallen ill, so we had to draft in our roadie Paul Fallon to stand in for Craig in the walking long shots of the band. You can spot him if you look closely.

A few years after we had recorded it, the chorus of the song seemed to have been 'borrowed' from by James Destri in his song 'Maria', recorded by Blondie. This similarity was so evident that when the Blondie song was a hit in the United States in 1999, some Inspirals fans contacted us asking why it was that they had covered one of our singles.

### Lovegrove

A sixties-influenced Graham song which gets its name from an episode of the Patrick McGoohan television show *Danger Man* called 'The Ubiquitous Mr Lovegrove', which is seen as a precursor to his psychedelic pièce de résistance, *The Prisoner*. The episode concerns a dream-like sequence, which follows a car crash suffered by the central character John Drake and a mysterious character who keeps turning up in the narrative.

### Just Wednesday

Composed by Clint, this is a witty yet sad song that sets the rigours of pop stardom against the personal trauma of a domestic dispute. It does so beautifully. 'I dreamed I saw a million people dancing, to some tune me and someone else were chanting. I woke in time to hear the front door slamming.'

*Saturn 5*

This song tells the love story that brought Clint's American wife Meagan Sheehan's mother and father together. ZEKE 64 was the registration of the motorbike that her father rode; the Rockettes were the dance troupe from the Radio City Music Hall that Meagan's aunt danced at in the sixties. Set against these images taken from the Sheehan's personal family photographs are the popular culture images of the space rocket delivery system, the Saturn V vehicle, man landing on the moon, and the assassination of John F. Kennedy. A clever, witty song, the message of which still reverberates now when people hear it at a club.

We filmed the video for 'Saturn 5' in Dallas at the Museum of Nature & Science where Zoë Ball came and filmed us on location for the BBC1 pop programme, *The Ozone*. She was very striking looking and we were impressed that she was the daughter of TV presenter Johnny Ball. We were also filmed by MTV while we were there, and the head of MTV Europe casually ordered $40 glasses of port. Nice work if you can get it.

*All Of This And More*

This is one of Martyn's songs and is another garage classic, recorded in the fresher new approach in line with the new album.

*The Way The Light Falls*

This was written by Clint and has a spare wistful groove to it, which is infectious. It appears to discuss the subject of fame, missing your loved ones, and straying from the path of virtue. 'Look what it's doing to me, see what this monster's doing to me.' It has a Doors-ish quality, in the lazy Fender Rhodes-style keyboard sound Clint used, and the insistent beat.

## Half Way There

This one was written largely by myself. It is another brash rock song which takes a refrain from the Charles & Eddie song 'Would I Lie To You?' but says, rather candidly, 'Yes, I probably would.' This song can now be seen partly as me writing a positive song that was saying in its message that the band had a lot more life in it, a future, a lot more albums and gigs. Unfortunately events went on to show that it wasn't to work out like that.

## Cobra

This was another song by Martyn. It was recorded pretty much live, and without a click track, in order that the rhythm could speed up and slow down, and we could get away from the automaton nature of the technological recording of songs like 'Dragging Me Down' and 'Two Worlds Collide'.

## I Don't Want To Go Blind

I composed the words and music to this one, originally on a keyboard. It is a sad soul song, and closes the last original Inspiral Carpets album. The words are quite fitting when you look at it with twenty-twenty hindsight. 'It's all just second hand dreams return to haunt you and me. I don't want to go blind.'

The *Devil Hopping* album came out in May 1994 and reached No. 10. The performance of the album and the singles from it weren't too bad: 'Saturn 5' was a popular hit, and reached No. 20, 'I Want You' reached No. 18. Daniel Miller was insistent that the next single should be 'Uniform'. We weren't that keen to have it as a single, but Daniel just went ahead and got the Balanescu Quartet to provide a string arrangement to play over my original vocal. When the single came out, it gained no radio airplay, and the expensive American-based promotional video didn't get played on *The Chart Show* before the all-important week of release. Consequently, the single bombed at No. 51. Daniel was correct in that it was a good song, but in my opinion it was jinxed and forcing us to release it went along with the general feeling of trouble during the whole of the album cycle from writing to inception, to recording, promotion and release.

# 27

## I think you should remember
## whose side you are on

When recording *Devil Hopping* we decided to avoid the
usual marketing-driven exercise of commissioning pointless,
generic, gratuitous dance remixes of the A- and B-sides
of potential singles. Instead we decided to exploit the fact
that Mute had booked Studio One of Parr Street Studios
in Liverpool as a lock-out for three weeks, with a view to
choosing a couple of singers that the whole band admired,
and getting them in to sing alternative versions of our songs.
There are very few bands and singers that every member of
Inspiral Carpets actually liked, but two bands that fell into
this category were Yargo and The Fall. I agreed to speak to
Basil, lead singer of Yargo, while Clint volunteered to get
the infamous Mark E. Smith on board.

Yargo were a tight, punky, funky, political, bluesy band,
fronted by Basil Clarke. I had seen them play at the PSV
club in Hulme and also at an outside gig somewhere near
the Town Hall in 1988. Basil had an unmistakable voice and
talent. When he sang he sounded a bit like Bob Marley, with
a Caribbean/Manchester accent, and he had a tonality to
his voice whereby the manipulation of the vowel sounds, of
tightening and loosening, were like a jazz trumpeter using a
mute to shape the sound of the notes escaping.

It was my job to pick Basil up from his house in Moss
Side, and drive him to the studio in Liverpool. While I was
driving round a roundabout in Manchester, there was a hint

that Basil's life might be lived a little more dangerously than mine. In front of us was a car where I could see two small children playing soldiers through the car's rear window, using their fingers to shoot at all the cars in their wake. I said to Basil, 'Look at those kids with guns,' and he immediately ducked down low in the seat as if we were under attack by a Manchester gang. I felt really bad.

Clint was given the more difficult quarry of Mark E. Smith. We knew his manager at the time, and Clint arranged to call Mark up to discuss contributing to a song. Mark said that he would sing along to two tracks, and that one would be a ballad, and the other would be spoken-word narrative. He agreed to do both for a small amount of money, which was very reasonable considering that he is such a legend – one of the two original punk singers, who, along with John Lydon, altered the entire course of pop music in Britain over the last thirty or so years. Better than a faceless remix then.

We spoke to Mute, who were both simultaneously excited and wary about working with Mark, on the basis that he had a reputation for being awkward to deal with. In the same way that Mrs Beeton began a section of her cookery book by entreating the cook to 'first catch your hare' when instructing them on how to cook hare stew, Mute presented us with some guarantees that we had to achieve before they would accept Mark E. Smith guesting on an Inspiral Carpets record. Firstly they wanted Mark to do a promotional video; press interviews with *NME* and *Melody Maker*; and, funniest of all, a *Top of the Pops* appearance, should an appropriate chart position from the prospective record be achieved.

Our hare having been caught, we arranged for Mark to come over to Parr Street in Liverpool to record a couple of songs. Pascal wasn't keen on us working with Mark E. Smith, arguing that he had earned a bad reputation in the business. A typical week recording in Liverpool would run from Monday morning until Friday afternoon, working eight-hour days. On Friday evening, Pascal would take a train back down to his wife and kids in London, so the American engineer, Clif Norrell, a highly respected producer in his own right, would stay in Liverpool, recording the B-sides and alternative vocal versions over the weekend.

Mark was supposed to have made the trip from Manchester to arrive at the studio for five o'clock. When he hadn't arrived by six, we began to think that he wasn't coming. There was an American man working in the reception of the studio, and at six thirty he rang through on the internal phone to inform us that, 'There is a Mr Smith in reception asking for you to pay a £55 taxi bill. Are you expecting him?'

Clint went to reception and brought Mark and his twenty-year-old girlfriend into the control room. Mark instantly read Pascal's antagonism towards him, but also picked up on his Belgian accent and quizzed, 'Where were your parents in 1940?' Pascal responded quickly, 'In the Belgian resistance.' After this welcoming exchange, Pascal packed his bags and hopped on a train to London.

Mark made himself at home, sitting down and listening to the two tracks we wanted him to sing on via a handheld, mono, tape-dictation machine. Mark sat there, with a big bag of pink base on the table in front of him, screwing his eyes up in concentration, listening to the tracks and saying surprising subjective comments like, 'The hi-hat cymbal is too loud in the mix.' How he could hear that on the distorted, mashed-up sound that was coming from the tape machine, I will never know.

Mark and his girlfriend left the studio and tried to book into the Adelphi Hotel. The staff there accused him, unfairly, of having a stolen credit card and wouldn't allow him to book a room, so the two of them came back and slept in the studio.

On the Saturday, Mark began to sing along to our new song, 'Saturn 5'. He growled his way through it. Only Clint, Clif and I were in the control room. I was very excited as Mark was shouting and emoting, and Clint, quite correctly, had to tell me to shut up in case Mark took umbrage at my laughter and hysteria. Pascal had a highly valuable and rare forties German ribbon microphone which was worth a couple of grand, and was so sensitive that it reputedly needed to be plugged in for a day before being used. I suggested to Clif that perhaps it might be best if we unplugged it and hid it away from harm, which he did. It was a good job as within twenty minutes Mark had shouted into the Uher microphone so loud that he had broken the ribbon. Clif found a cheaper Shure SM58 and we carried on.

Once Mark had sung ten passes of 'Saturn 5', I persuaded Clint that Mark should have a go at singing on Martyn's song 'I Want You', as it struck me as being a more natural song for him to contribute to, being so fast and aggressive, with plenty of aggressive drums and distorted guitar.

Mark was singing in the studio and suddenly he shouted something to me, but I couldn't work out if it was a statement or a question: 'Back, Tom? You back, Tom?' I couldn't fathom what Mark was getting at, especially as Martyn had written the lyrics. Clint, however, realised that Mark was asking if he could add the word 'back' to the chorus line, 'I want you', as a way of demarcating his version from the original Inspirals version.

Once Mark had done a few passes on 'I Want You', we thanked him and he hopped on a train back to Manchester. Clint and Clif edited a patchwork of all the vocal performances Mark had done. 'I Want You – Back' sounded like a classic, with Mark adding a whole host of themes to the song, including an attack on his American record company, 'The Dutch East India Company in the USA of A think they can fool me with their sincere usury'; the delightful romantic couplet, 'You say you lost ten stone in weight… so what did you look like fat?' and the threatening opener, 'I think you should remember whose side you are on.' We decided that Mark's version of 'I Want You' was head and shoulders above his take on 'Saturn 5'.

Inspirals wanted the video for the song to be filmed at Bernard Manning's Embassy Club in Harpurhey, the idea being that Mark would dress up in a suit and bow tie, and introduce the band at the beginning of the video as if he was some Northern comedian. We also wanted some girls to mob us in the video, as a parody of pop videos. Mute, as ever the indie, baulked at the first hurdle. They insisted on the video being filmed on the stage of Brixton Academy, possibly scared that the Manning connotation might brand the band as racist. They did agree to book some models to appear in the video, but instead of mobbing us, they got them to attack us. The video production company brought along a variety of clothes for us to wear. Mark ended up in a £600 shiny Italian designer suit.

After upsetting the lady at the small hotel in Swiss Cottage by being rude, Mark started drinking at 8:00am, chiselling away at a bottle of Newcastle Brown Ale while smoking Regals. We arrived at Brixton Academy and started filming at 10:00am. A regular video shoot for Inspirals at this time cost in the region of £30k and would involve a crew comprising cameramen, lighting technicians, props, catering and a director. We'd be filmed approximately thirty times, from different angles, using different lengths of shot, with sweeps and flourishes created by using cranes and dollies.

Mark, being an eccentric, quite often adopted an extreme position or mode of behaviour, especially when asked to carry out a specific task that he wasn't keen on doing. He attempted to bring the video shoot to an end after just two takes of the song by launching the SM58 microphone in his hand straight into the cameraman's eye. Said eyeball swelled like Popeye, post-spinach. A ghastly hush descended over proceedings and we all wondered what might happen next. In an act of defiance and total professionalism (and probably in the spirit of not letting Mark get his own way) the injured man ignored the physical provocation and said, 'Right let's get on with the next shot.'

Mark was persuaded to stay the full length of the video shoot by the rest of us bribing him with a mixture of alcohol, cannabis, speed and jokes. At the end of the shoot, Mark tried to walk off, still donning the Italian suit, which by this time was decorated with piss stains round the crotch. The stylist had to chase him in and out of Brixton pubs to retrieve it.

It was customary for me to lend the band my Toyota Previa people carrier for promotional trips. Something told me to hire a similar vehicle for the two or three trips we made with Mark down to London and back. This instinct served me well as, on each occasion, by the time we got back to Manchester, Mark, through what I believe was carelessness and not design, had managed to burn a succession of cigarette burns into the seats.

I think that Mark was used to ruling the roost in The Fall, getting away with behaving in any way he saw fit, often challenging everyone in his entourage and ever upping the ante. He couldn't get away with behaving that way with our gang, because we treated him as an equal. He could bully away, but at some point the Inspirals group dynamic would kick in.

Being the goading kind, Mark once accused Craig of trying to curry favour with him by pretending to drink a can of beer when it was actually empty. Craig said there was, indeed, beer in his can, and that he would have to prove that there was if Mark repeated his false claim. Mark then repeated the accusation, and Craig emptied half a can of beer over his head.

When 'I Want You' was released, the hilarious video got played on the all-important *Chart Show*, essential for any indie success at that time. The *NME* made our record their single of the week and when the song entered the charts at No. 18, we were asked to appear on *Top of the Pops*.

Our radio and television plugger, Nicki Kefalas from Out Promotions, was at the studio to keep an eye on us, ensure that the filming went well, and to make sure that we didn't upset the producer and thereby make it harder for other clients that they represented. Mark ignored Nicki, and she didn't like him or the threat he represented.

*Top of the Pops* was recorded on a Wednesday or Thursday at Elstree Studios and was transmitted on a Friday night at 7 o'clock. The recording would start at 9:00am. The director would be unseen, in an observation room above the ceiling, and would communicate via headphones with the floor manager who would conduct the lighting and cameraman on the studio floor. On the first run-through, the band would mime along to the song while I sang a live vocal, and the combination of the director, the floor manager, camera crew and lighting would run through the song, establishing camera angles, special effects, edits, song titles and how the section we were featured in would run into the next piece of the show.

Once the production crew gained the camera angles and camera edits for each performing artist by processing them on their own without the rest of the performers being present, they would then progress by getting everyone to run through their song as a joined-up segment of the whole show as a dry run, with the cameras present, but not actually filming. A third run-through would be done with make-up and costume, with the edits and camera angles and presenters in place and a trial recording would be made. During a final run-through, the show would be recorded as one continual performance, with all edits and special effects in place. Because of the nature of this process, reliability and consistency were vital in each performing unit. If you fluffed your words, swore, or stopped, you could be making everyone else in the studio have to redo their performance – some pressure then. I didn't mind singing a live vocal, having little fear in my ability to perform under pressure, and in one way or another, I had been rehearsing a long time to be on this particular TV show.

We used to do mimed backings and live vocals on *Top of the Pops* and I was a safe pair of lungs, as far as pre-records and live records were concerned. I've always prided myself on being able to nail pre-recorded singing or live TV performances confidently and reliably, so that Inspiral Carpets would get invited to record as many TV music programmes as possible. And we did plenty. We once appeared on *Friday Night At The Dome*, filmed at The National in Kilburn in London, and Lenny Kravitz watched us rehearsing 'The Wind Is Calling Your Name' in the afternoon, a few hours before the live audience were allowed in. He approached me after the full run-through and said, 'With a voice like that, you should be singing on Broadway' – a nice rock and roll moment for me, even if he was just being friendly. Once on *Later with Jools Holland* we refused to take part in the hippy communal jam at the beginning of the show, partly because it was our duly appointed role to be the grumpy indie band on the show, but I'm also not sure that we had the technical musical ability to actually join in, improvise and contribute.

*Top of the Pops* was a programme that I always imagined myself appearing on, even as a child miming in our neighbour Will's attic playroom with a tennis racket. I never really doubted that one day I would tread those boards. In total,

Inspiral Carpets appeared nine times on *Top of the Pops*, twice with the singles 'This Is How It Feels' and 'She Comes In The Fall', and once with 'Generations', 'Caravan', 'Dragging Me Down', 'Saturn 5' and 'I Want You'.

The dichotomy between the way that fans enjoyed and experienced *Top of the Pops* and the reality of filming the show was quite strange, but I always enjoyed the difference between the two. I remember when we appeared on the show for the first time and the effect it had when Alison and I went to a club in Chester the following weekend – everyone in the place was talking to me as if they knew me.

All the appearances, up until the last two singles, were filmed at Broadcasting House at Wood Lane, Shepherd's Bush – the iconic building where other famous shows, such as *Blue Peter* and *The Goodies* were filmed. For some reason, the BBC now want to bulldoze Broadcasting House. In twenty years time people will be asking why they knocked down this cultural artefact, as they do about the Cavern in Liverpool, or Oasis' rehearsal room within The Boardwalk in Manchester.

It was a weird set-up at Wood Lane. Commissionaires manned the gate to the entrance and, in the true flavour of civil-service broadcasting, if you reacted to their officiousness with even a modicum of humour or rudeness, you weren't coming in and you weren't appearing on *Top of the Pops*.

There was a funny hierarchy at the BBC at that time. If you were a big star or in a big pop band, you would be allowed to mime the lead vocal, but if you were in an indie band you were expected to show your authenticity by singing the lead vocal live against the backing track. I guess that was to lend the programme some element of live performance, and it was also because at the back of your mind, there was always the idea that the director of the programmes never really wanted you to be on the show in the first place, and if you stepped out of line you would be bounced off the show quicker than Mariah Carey could have a diva strop.

When we filmed *Top of the Pops* with Mark E. Smith, he brought a friend called Brian with him. Brian seemed innocuous enough and Mark claimed that he was his hairdresser, although darker voices in our entourage whispered that he was a black belt in Judo and not to be messed with. Mark thought nothing of trying, at every possible turn, to get us to have our hair cut by him, an offer we persistently declined.

We did the first run-through and Mark was being relatively well behaved, at least by his previous form. I think that even he was excited about appearing on this flagship iconic British pop show, and the absurdity of it all. Mark, ever the 'professional', had all his lyrics handwritten on a piece of paper. During the first run-through he performed the song as though it was 'Rock Around the Clock', all fast and furious. By the second run-through, he performed his contributions slow and relaxed – a bit more like 'Bright Eyes'.

This would probably have been a real problem to the production crew, who would have viewed Mark's spontaneity as him performing the song inconsistently. This jarred with their values of how bands should be captured for mainstream BBC1 consumption. As far as they were concerned, the performance should stay the same each time, consistent and familiar like the speed of the conveyor belt on the *Generation Game*, or the size of Eric Morecambe's glasses. Mark offended their public service idea of rock and roll and pop music, and created a ripple of shock. It was as if something uncomfortable had entered their rarefied broadcasting universe, as though the presenter of the *Antiques Road Show* had sat down and taken a shit on a William and Mary table in front of the Queen at Buckingham Palace.

194

At this point Nicki called the whole of the band over and said, 'The producer doesn't like Mark. He wants you to perform the song without him.' This put us in a difficult position. After having 'caught our hare', we were now being asked to bump Mark (the reason for all the success happening) out of the way. Nice. Moving the goalposts as usual, putting us in the place of having to tell Mark that 'we' didn't want him on the show. What nonsense.

Clint was prepared to do the show without Mark, if it prevented us from alienating our record company and promotions staff. I insisted, with Graham's support, that we dug our heels in and did the show with Mark. The other option was to fuck it off and tell them where to stick their show.

So, we filmed 'I Want You' with Mark E. Smith, and it was such a hilarious performance that the BBC even repeated it on their Saturday-morning kids' show, with whatever furry animal-themed puppet they had co-presenting the clip, mocking Mark's lyrics, handwritten on paper, and in shot.

During that day's filming I managed to upset Elvis Costello. I saw him walking down one of the long corridors at Elstree with his drummer and his bass player, Bruce Thomas. I had recently been reading an article in Q magazine about early Fleetwood Mac guitarist and blues mastermind Peter Green. In the interview, Bruce had been relating a story that, as a fifteen-year-old, he had hitched down to London to audition to be in an early version of what became Fleetwood Mac, and that Green had told him that he was 'playing too many notes' for blues. When I met the three of them I shook their hands and recounted this story. I don't think Elvis liked being upstaged by his bass player. I love Elvis Costello and his records, and I went to see him play in the New Theatre in Oxford in 1978 when This Year's Model had just been released, but I love Peter Green more.

Later in the day, when Inspirals and Mark were in the make-up department waiting to do our final run-through, Elvis and his band were in the green room, just yards from us, and they were watching their run-through. As their song ended, the overzealous American drummer ran up to the floor manager and begged for them to re-shoot their take because, although the vocals were live and the band were miming to a backing tape, there was a bit on the last beat of the song where the hi-hat stand fell over. Mark, ever the diplomat, pulled himself up square to the American and said in pure Salford, 'There's no point doing it again, it was shit when you did it the first time and it will be just as shit if you do it again.' The prospect of two of the more senior men of the punk/new wave movement scrapping was almost too enjoyable, but the moment passed and it didn't happen. However, during one of the run-throughs, Clint and Mark had an altercation and punched each other.

While we were waiting for our final run-through, Mark got a speed frenzy and started getting all the rubbish in the dressing room together – all the paper plates, polystyrene cups, bits of food and plastic bottles – he put everything on a tray, got one of the band to open the door and then he threw it out without looking. Unfortunately, at the same moment, Anita Doth, the female singer from 2 Unlimited, was walking past the door and it went all over her. The door closed, and when Clint reopened it a few seconds later, amidst stifled laughter we saw poor Nicki on all-fours picking up all the detritus. Later, Mark cheekily got Martyn to ask Anita if she liked him and fancied a date.

The final story from this eventful recording of *Top of the Pops* happened when we had filmed our segment, and had got the all clear from the director, via the floor manager, and gone into the bar in Elstree. In the bar was a ragbag of pop musicians and actors from *EastEnders*. While we were sitting there, Gillian Taylforth brushed through with her kids. One of the kids unfortunately tripped up over Mark's extended foot. Acting like she owned the place, Gillian turned to Mark and said, 'Aren't you going to apologise to my kid? Haven't you got any manners?' to which Mark looked to his friend, Brian, and said in a stage whisper full of menace, 'Hey, Brian, why don't you go up to the dressing room and get those cut-throat razors, then we can sort this out.'

Within six months of this, Inspiral Carpets were dropped by Mute Records. If they had wanted us, they didn't want us anymore. At the end of the year 'I Want You' topped John Peel's Festive Fifty.

# 28

## Dreams are all we have

Steven Hawkins was an eccentric music aficionado from Yorkshire who tour managed us for a lot of 1993. Steven was a nice person, but he wasn't the best organiser in the world. He was not a great believer in maps and when we were on the tour bus he would demarcate the directions of left and right as being 'left' (left) and 'soft left' (right). Steven seemed to enjoy getting paid by us to see the world, but wasn't concerned about whether we could actually afford to pay ourselves a wage, keep the business going and pay our bills.

A typical Steven booking was two Icelandic shows he organised. The trip took two unproductive travel days to get there, plus two back, yet the gig fees were only slightly more than the cost of the ferry. To spare Steven's feelings, I cancelled the shows with our agent Charlie Myatt at 13 Artists, and asked him to tell Steven that the promoter had pulled the gigs.

We turned up to play a university ball at Porto in Portugal and for once felt very pleased to be getting paid £6,000 for such an obscure show. But when 10,000 Portuguese punters turned up to see us play, we discovered that our single 'Please Be Cruel' had been a top 10 hit on the college import chart and Steven had therefore negotiated a rubbish deal. At the same show, Steven was leaning absent-mindedly against a box in the enormous sports hall where we were playing, and asked the promoter bluntly where the mixing desk for the PA was. The promoter replied, dumbfounded in his second language, that Steven was leaning on it.

We once did a skit across the world, taking in Japan, New York and Europe, leaving a trail of debt everywhere we went. At a gig in Japan there was a stage invasion after which the promoter claimed we had *invited* the audience on stage and caused £11,000 worth of damage. We played three shows in Greece, one in Thessalonica and two in Athens. In the past these shows generally made us about £10,000. This time, however, we flew out of Frankfurt airport without having made any provision to pre-book the backline and amazingly heavy keyboards on a cheap freight price. When we got to Athens I had to get my credit card out to pay the excess charge of £1,600: un-budgeted, un-planned and ridiculous. We can't have come home with more than £6,000.

We performed some shows with The Levellers in Germany. For the first gig, Steven booked us onto a cheap flight that landed some 90 miles away from the festival. A guy from the gig taxied us in a butcher's van which wasn't big enough for us all, and there was blood, guts and giblets on the floor. Craig and I sat in the back with a grill up against our faces as we raced towards the gig where we were billed to be appearing 60 minutes later.

The gig was taking place outside a sports centre and our dressing room was a disused bowling alley with a lot of trophy cups at one end and bowling lanes at the other. Mark, the singer from The Levellers, came in to see us, so we prepared the dressing room for him. Graham suggested that Mark have a go at bowling a ball down the lane. The lights were turned down low and you couldn't see much, but Mark took an enormous swing and threw the heavy ball fast down the bowling alley. It ran smoothly down the channel for five seconds and then mysteriously stopped before rolling back at twice the original speed and velocity. Graham said something about the bowling alley being haunted, and Mark laughed, made his goodbyes and went back outside into the

German summer sun. Only then did Craig crawl back out from his hiding place, 60 feet into the alley.

After the show, our German record company licensee Erik van Kassen came to see us in our bowling alley. Eric had always fought our corner where release and promotion was concerned, and we sold a lot of records in Germany, sometimes 12,000 per release, in no small part thanks to him. Graham pissed in one of the bowling trophies and then poured beer in. When Erik came in, Graham offered him the beer in the trophy, and I shouted a warning, but Erik didn't believe me and drank it anyway. It took about a third of a second for his face to break from the pre-drink smile.

Later on that tour we played at the Roskilde Festival. Clint got really drunk and started doing handstands in the goldfish-inhabited ponds that were backstage. A hippy hand came up and asked him to stop doing it, as it was considered animal cruelty and they were the same fish who had graced the backstage area every year since it began in 1972, started by two school friends.

Once we had performed, The Levellers went on. Craig was in a devilish, drunken mood and decided that he was going to bum-rush the stage and pull The Levellers' drummer off his stool, mid-song. He ran up onto the stage very fast and we followed him, but when we got up there, Craig was transfixed by watching the audience of some 80,000 people going mental to The Levellers. If Craig hadn't understood the allure of the band before that moment, he did now.

ZZ Top were playing after The Levellers. Clint walked up and disturbed them in the middle of an *MTV* heavy metal guitar giveaway competition. He sat himself between the two bearded ones and, belching, lent over to one and said, 'Can I have your autograph, Billy?' In an annoyed Southern drawl, the musician said, 'I'm Dusty... that's Billy over there.'

Back at the hotel, we watched an England football match,

and I got very drunk. At one point the rest of the band dangled me out of a 4th-storey window, head first, by my legs. I trusted them, though, and didn't make too much fuss while Graham and Clint posed questions such as 'I wonder how much insurance money we would get if we dropped him and killed him?' The next day I woke up after having blacked out through drinking. This is one of only two times this has ever happened, and I didn't like the idea of it.

After that trip we huddled into the Cow office with Brenda, and she put together all the receipts and calculated that, after some four months of hard slog, we had just about broken even.

With Steven politely sacked, we got on with the job of trying to find a new band manager to take us through to the fifth album. After some soul searching, we settled on Peter Felstead at CEC Management. Peter had another string to his bow in that he ran Nude Records along with his business partner Saul Galpern, the label for wonderful bands such as Suede, Goya Dress and Geneva.

In the sixties, aged eighteen and fresh to the business, Peter was working for the publishers Blue Mountain Music. His boss had left him on his own to look after the famously difficult and grumpy Roy Orbison. The Big O had gone to a Bentley garage in Hampstead and had been looking at the brand new cars. The salesman was a bit rude and sniffy to him, so Roy, ever aware of a slight, told Peter to get £25,000 in cash so that they could come back and buy one of the expensive cars outright to make a point that you can't judge a book by its cover, and probably just because he could. Peter rang up his boss and asked him what he should do, but his boss had no idea. Peter said that they had probably better do what Orbison wanted them to do, so Blue Mountain Music had to arrange for the enormous amount of money to be picked up from a bank. Peter went back to the garage with the singer and bought the car from the snobby salesman. Curiously, the comedian and comedy writer Ricky Gervais once managed Suede and he must have knocked about the CEC office a bit. He created a similar scene in the *Extras* Christmas special, possibly inspired by Peter's story.

I got the distinct impression that Daniel Miller didn't like the idea of Peter Felstead managing us. For some reason Daniel often didn't like artist managers – maybe he felt they interfered with his artistic vision of building up a boutique indie label like Mute. Pascal Gabriel was very matey with Daniel, but we'd decided that we didn't want to extend our recording career with Pascal at the helm, as I think we felt that, creatively, we had wrung that particular lemon dry.

Peter Felstead's first job was to negotiate with Mute about picking up our fifth option and paying us an advance. His second job was to petition prospective parties for the production job. Finding producers is always difficult, and it's hard to know who might want to produce an album by a band whose last three albums had sold progressively less.

We sat in the plush London offices of CEC management and auditioned four separate prospective producers. The first was a young man called Chris Sheldon, an ex-drummer who was currently working with the eccentric and wonderful band Talk Talk. He told us that he had been attempting to write a song with the perfectionist band member Mark Hollis, and they had spent three weeks composing a verse and a chorus. After a further week, Mark was unhappy with the chorus, so they had come up with a new one, then he was unhappy with the verse, so they spent a week creating a new verse. This went on and on until the entire song had been recreated several times and Chris gave up. He seemed like a personable man, but maybe not assertive enough for a noisy, assertive bunch like Inspiral Carpets.

The next producer who came in was an old punk called Dave Charles, who had produced The La's album. In 1975, he had been the engineer on Dr. Feelgood's debut album *Down by the Jetty*, the first album I bought and still one of my favourites. I was impressed, but as soon as he sat down he started laying into me, saying that I was lazy and my singing was shit and, from the evidence of Inspiral Carpets' previous albums' sonic qualities and decreasing sales performance, that I was a problem. Immediately, Craig joined in saying that indeed I was lazy, and could make more effort. Nice touch that.

To be fair on Dave Charles, I think he was testing the band to see if we had any more fire left in our bellies. For all I know, he was trying to investigate whether it was worth Mute picking up their final, fifth album option, and if it was worth him devoting effort and time to a band that had already had it and were on their way to the scrapheap. He might have been testing our gang mentality. If he was, we had failed the test: Craig had insulted me in the process and I wouldn't have worked with Dave Charles for all the tea in China, even if he had contributed to one of my all-time favourite records.

Next in was Tim Friese-Greene, long time member of Talk Talk and, more importantly, producer of Tight Fit's eighties No. 1 hit 'The Lion Sleeps Tonight'. It was lovely to meet Tim, but he came across a bit Dr Who, slurring his words in a druggy way. I was sure that he was at a crossroads in his professional career, and that he may have turned up to the meeting purely because he needed work. His drawl was piss-taking and ironic, he was saying stuff like, 'I only want to work in a studio where the kitchen has cat food in a bowl which has been in it for three days.' I am not sure if Tim felt that we were expecting to meet a mad auteur genius and he was acting to a character he had created for our benefit.

Suddenly, mid-sentence, he stopped talking, stood up like the white rabbit in *Alice in Wonderland* and said, 'I just need to go to the toilet.' He walked out of the office, out of the building, and we tracked him out of the window as he walked down the street and disappeared from view.

I think I preferred the experience of being insulted by Dave Charles: at least it was something you could get angry and react to; this was just strange behaviour.

Ed Buller, in comparison, seemed relatively normal and we got on with him. Ed had been a session keyboard player for The Psychedelic Furs and had produced three albums by Suede. He was in the studio when the legendary bust up took place between guitarist Bernard Butler and singer Brett Anderson. We arranged for Peter Felstead to talk to Mute about booking him for a recording session in Britannia Row in Islington for the autumn of 1994.

It was to be a disaster.

Mute hadn't picked up the option for the fifth album in our deal. What they agreed to do was to fund a prospective recording session, and to decide later if the recordings sounded like they were hit material. Mute agreed to pay for the Britannia Row studio for two weeks, and for Buller's extortionate production fee.

In the summer of 1994, Daniel arranged to meet the band at Kai's, a Chinese restaurant in Manchester's Chinatown. It was an eatery that I used to go to in the mid-eighties after a night of glass collecting at the Haçienda, because it had a Buddhist-inspired tofu menu where you could eat bean curd coloured and textured to look like pork, beef or chicken. This is what brought the vegetarian Daniel Miller to this particular restaurant ten years later.

Bearing in mind that it was a business meeting and that no one from CEC Management would be there, we needed to stay guarded. Before the meeting I suggested two tactical measures to the other band members. The first measure was that we shouldn't get drunk because, although we were very fond of Daniel, he was, at the end of the day, a business associate, and not ultimately a friend. The second stratagem was that no one out of the band should suggest that the label issue a greatest hits compilation.

Most record deals contain within them a clause that says that the label can drop the artist, stop paying them an advance, and then issue a greatest hits compilation. My argument was that, at this difficult time for Inspiral Carpets, unless we projected an air of confidence about a new phase and new songs, Mute would drop us and put out a hits record. In this context, for us to suggest one would be career suicide. An hour and a half into the meal, Craig, high on the atmosphere and Tsingtao, suggested to Daniel that Inspiral Carpets should release a greatest hits record, and four months later my prediction was realised.

The Britannia Row session took place in September 1994 in the studio where Joy Division had recorded the album *Closer*. We wrote about fifteen songs, turned up at the studio and began a fortnight recording session. It has the dubious accolade of being pretty much the only recording session Inspiral Carpets ever did where not a single note of material was ever released.

Ed Buller would turn up to the studio at two in the afternoon because his wife was expecting their first baby. Quite often he would sit around, record an idea for a song and then go home at about six in the evening. Not bad for a thousand pounds a day. Ed at that point was one of a select group of collectors of old Moog synthesisers. Daniel Miller was another, and so Daniel would come in to the studio and talk serious synth with Ed.

The recording session quickly descended into farce. We did more recording with the engineer than with Ed, who spent a lot of the little time he was there arguing with Graham about any irrelevance. They once argued about whether Phil Collins was an authentic artist and performer. Ed was arguing that he was shit, and Graham, for whatever perverse reason, was defending him.

We recorded half a dozen songs, including one that Martyn wrote called 'No Fun No More'. Ed used the Moog synth to create a big pounding beat and the words were spat over the guitars, drums and keyboards. It sounded a little like the goth metal band Ministry.

When the session had ended, we invited Daniel along to hear the tracks, hoping that it would herald him and Mute picking up the option for the album. I even went out on to Islington High Street and foolishly bought a couple of bottles of champagne from a posh off-licence. We listened to the tracks in the control room and then had a meal at which Daniel was very quiet and non-committal about the future.

On 24th October 1994 I received a phone call from Julian de Takats from CEC with the news that Mute had decided to pass on the fifth album option, and had effectively dropped Inspiral Carpets, almost exactly five years after they had won the scramble to sign us.

We did one last recording session in Suite 16 in Rochdale in 1995, for which our publishers Mute Song put up the money. The idea was to record something successfully after the Ed Buller fiasco, and to do it cheap and locally, the polar opposite of the previous session. An engineer called Stuart James ran the sessions, and guess what? We actually got some recording done – amazing. I even played electric guitar on a couple of songs. It was a fun, pleasant session; a coda to a long, mostly successful writing and recording career for Inspiral Carpets, although we didn't know that at the time.

# 29

## The jewels you sell
## are the finest in the world

Inspiral Carpets were a band that made money from recording and from songwriting. Record deals make money from the actual sound recordings and not the songs themselves. To make money from the songs, there is a separate publishing deal.

It used to be a business maxim that it's not a good idea to sign a record and publishing deal with the same company, for a variety of reasons. Firstly, record companies have to pay the royalty to the publishing company, and if they are the same company they may hide sales or under-report income. Secondly, making recordings is an expensive business, while publishing is basically a banking operation where you collect money from other people – PRS for Music, publishing from record companies etc. If you have one company handling both recording and publishing, they may drop you as a recording artist, but retain you as songwriters if they can't make enough money from sales of your albums – it increases their power over you and reduces your negotiating position.

The first publishing deal we were offered was in 1989 by Empire Music, the people behind China Records who signed The Levellers. They offered us a £9,000 advance for a five album publishing deal. Binsey was keen to secure some cash flow at a difficult time when we had our own small independent label, Cow. However, we rejected the offer.

Once we had secured a proper record deal with Mute in 1989, we negotiated with three or four major publishers, including Virgin, Chrysalis and EMI. In one meeting, we were asked how big an advance we were expecting, to which our posh lawyer Tony English said, in full received pronunciation, '250 Big Ones!' The A&R man from Chrysalis replied that £250,000 was a little more than they were expecting to commit to corporately. Tony replied, mischievously, 'They are terribly hard-working, Northern working-class lads, if they say they want 250 big ones I am sure that's the market value.'

So, we signed and they paid us £125,000 upon signing, and another £125,000 upon release of the debut album, *Life,* in April 1990. Our lawyer Tony had sewn up a fantastic publishing deal on our behalf. I used to affectionately refer to him as our own personal Exocet missile, in that his service cost a million quid, but you could point him at a distant object and he would destroy it utterly, and with absolute precision.

Something that had very much attracted us to Chrysalis was their A&R man, Stuart Slater. He had been the lead singer of The Mojos, and Bowie covered his song 'Everything's Alright' on his 1973 *Pin Ups* album, which added quite a bit of weight and credibility to his opinion about our songwriting careers.

Chrysalis signed us for a five album publishing deal, which tracked the record deal we had with Mute. Tony had built in a success formula which meant that once the publisher picked up the subsequent albums, they would have to pay an advance that was higher than the initial one of £250,000. Our debut album *Life* quickly achieved sales of 100,000 copies – we all got gold records to celebrate it from the BPI – and it went on to sell well in territories including the US, Germany, Spain, France and South America, selling 400,000 copies worldwide. Chrysalis then paid us a total advance of £325,000 for our second album, *The Beast Inside*.

After the disappointment of *The Beast Inside*, Tony delivered the news that Chrysalis weren't going to pick up the publishing option for our third album. We were on a European tour in Germany at the time, it was near Christmas and I was buying toys for my daughter, including a brightly painted tin roundabout with clockwork tin horses that spun round while playing a tune. I was speaking to Tony on a pay phone when he broke this not very festive news. The loss in cash flow would have serious implications on the whole band and our families.

We entered the pre-release recording schedule for *Revenge of the Goldfish* with no publishing deal. Tony had negotiated such a watertight publishing contract with Chrysalis that upon dropping us they rescinded any rights on future, as yet unreleased, material. When our next single 'Dragging Me Down' chartered at No. 12, Chrysalis took the liberty of placing their name next to ours in the chart in the music industry publication *Music Week*, a right they no longer had. Tony called them and warned them with the threat of an injunction, unless they removed their name from the following week's chart. And so it did the following week, when the publisher appeared as Copyright Control next to our name and song title. This meant a loss of face by Chrysalis, who appeared to have dropped us at the wrong time.

Within a few hours, Chrysalis had come to heal and had offered a revised advance of £185,000 for the third Inspiral Carpets album, which was reduced from the original 1990 deal, but still more than respectable. When we attended the signing ceremony the following month at Chrysalis' HQ, an old converted brewery in Fulham, we were sat on the top balcony conversing with Chris Wright who asked

Craig what it was like living in 'Chadlington'? I think he meant Chadderton, the working-class district of Oldham where Craig hailed from. All I wanted to do was to get the ink dry on the cheque and get the fuck out of there before they checked their balance sheet and cancelled it. On the way back from the meeting, we gave Tony a lift in our van, and we tried to get him to break two laws simultaneously by showing him Kubrik's *A Clockwork Orange* – it was still illegal to watch the film in the UK at the time – and trying to get him to smoke cannabis, which he refused to do.

We didn't have a hit on a similar scale to 'Dragging Me Down' from the album *Revenge of the Goldfish* so Chrysalis dropped us a second time in 1993, leaving us without a publishing deal again. After a year of protracted negotiations, we eventually signed to the Mute publishing arm Mute Song Ltd. So, against our own sensible advice, we were left in the vulnerable position where our record company had both our recording contract and our publishing contract too. Other matters were going to produce a perfect storm for Inspiral Carpets over the summer and autumn of 1994.

# 30

## The snake is a charmer,
## can turn on its master

The way that our band operated was that we had a company that ran our music business, called Audiobeat Limited, of which we were all directors and had equal shares, as did our manager, Binsey Smith – until we booted him out in our legal altercation of 1992. Each director also had their own satellite limited company, which contracted its services to Audiobeat. A mistake we had in this business architecture was to have the same accountancy firm producing accounts and tax planning for both the communal and individual companies.

As a band, Inspiral Carpets were always fairly well organised: we kept appropriate records and filed tax returns. However, with the best will in the world, we were often late in submitting forms. Then again, I have always felt the music industry is peopled largely by fuckwits, and that the general level of probity is very low, possibly ranking somewhere just below whoring or drug dealing in most places.

Our first accountants were called Freedman Frankl & Taylor. We fired them in 1990 for not being proactive enough in our tax planning and dealings. We hired a bookkeeper called Stephanie to work in our office, to ensure that all the income was logged, banking was recorded and that all invoices were paid and recorded. In 1990 we moved over to a famous London music biz accountancy firm called OJK, who represented a group of well-known

Irish artists. We worked with two accountants there, one of whom was Mr P.

Stephanie moved on in 1991, and we were without a bookkeeper from late 1991 onwards. We got in trouble for late filing of accounts in 1991, and I had to sit with our London-based accountant to unpick our business tax liabilities.

In 1992 we had a meeting with Mr P. at OJK's offices, where we complained that our accountancy bills seemed very expensive. As a joke, Mr P. entered the meeting room brandishing a baseball bat, in what I can only surmise was a homage to *Spinal Tap*'s fictional manager Ian Faith's fabled belief of the baseball bat's positive contribution to negotiations – this was a little more 'Inspiral Tap', if you will! Mr P. was a warm, funny Irish man.

These vague rumblings that we were being charged a lot continued throughout 1992 and beyond, until Brenda Clegg became our bookkeeper. Brenda worked for us during the end of Binsey Smith's tenure. Once she had helped us remove Binsey, she turned her attentions to our accountants, stating that she didn't think they represented good value for money. Brenda suggested that we sack them. I warned her that, if we did, that they would pursue us for a lot of money as a response.

In the autumn of 1993, acting on Brenda's advice, we dispensed with OJK's services. In the return post we received a bill for both individual and communal accountancy for £40,000. We then got into a legal dispute with OJK where they exercised a procedure called a 'lien', which literally meant that they would sit on all the tax returns, invoices, and papers that they were holding on our behalf until the dispute over payment was resolved satisfactorily to them. This meant that, irrespective of what the Inland Revenue or Customs and Excise needed from us, we couldn't actually supply it.

We were hamstrung. We engaged our lawyers, Russells, to pick through the mess. It turned out that two of the band members/directors owed substantial monies for accounts that the firm had produced on their behalf for their own satellite companies, but for which they hadn't been paid. This blurring of payments for communal and individual services would not have looked good in a court of law because it made us look like late paying clients, which, overall, we weren't.

When we looked through the £40,000 bill, there seemed to be a few thousand pounds billed by the accountancy firm for the calculation of what we individually and communally owed, which didn't seem strictly fair, as some of the services they had billed us for had already been paid. Eventually these additions were removed. In what other profession (apart from law perhaps) are you charged thousands for the time it takes to compose your bill? A nice business to get into, I reckon.

It took a year, and about £20,000 in legal mediation to bring the bill down to roughly half of the original £40,000 figure, so it is arguable that we might have been better off just paying it in the first place. Once Mute had failed to pick up our fifth album option, we didn't have any cash flow, and we only actually had £40,000 in our collective bank accounts, so paying it would have cleaned us out, and we would have been skint! A fact that rankles me is that the tax office actually has an undertaking to produce accounts for any individual or company if you don't bother producing accounts with a chartered accountant, and just turn up with all your invoices and payments, un-constructed, on bits of paper in a shoebox. Sometimes I think it might have been cheaper and easier, even with the fines that we would've incurred. The storm clouds were gathering...

# 31

## I don't want to go blind

We weren't getting on that well as a band. I was obsessing about merchandise and the minutiae of Inspiral Carpets micromanagement and, unsurprisingly, it was irritating other band members. Managing ourselves with CEC wasn't working. We decided we'd do a run of very small shows, with the aim of thanking our long-suffering fans, and I suppose doing something that might, for once, be quite easy to succeed at doing. The tour was to be called 'Village Hopping'.

The run of small shows around the UK took us to the Lemon Tree in Aberdeen and Lucifer's Saw Mill in Dundee, where the venue was so small that Clint had to play on a separate stage on the other side of the walkway to the toilet, perhaps a premonition of the solo career that was to beckon. We played The Venue in Edinburgh, and TJ's in Newport, a spit-and-sawdust place that we played on the way up. There was a couple of concerts in Ireland, including one in a club in Waterford where we played to a confused-looking audience who were eating chicken in a basket, and didn't seem too impressed. We did a live interview on the local radio station where Craig said that he would do an impersonation of Kurt Cobain for them, and then imitated a lone shotgun cartridge exploding. It was very soon after the Nirvana singer had killed himself, and I think Craig probably enjoyed the joke more than the interviewer or the radio audience.

Our final concerts were abroad. Mute had arranged for us

214

to do a series of shows in the newly independent countries of Czech Republic and Slovenia, with Moby supporting. We met Moby in Slovenia when he got on the old seventies brown holiday coach that they used to drive us around. It looked like the one that the 'Carry On' crew took to the seaside in the film *Carry On at Your Convenience.* Moby at that time was a militant, vegetarian, anti-smoker and insisted at great American-length that no one should dare to smoke in front of his precious temple of a body. He objected so much to someone in our crew smoking outside the bus during a break that he crawled out of the sun roof onto the top of the bus, while it was being driven, and sat on the roof to avoid us and the risk of moral contamination.

Moby's sense of himself and the barriers of others was a wonder to behold, full of contradictions, paradoxes and certain hypocrisies. We shared a flight with Moby that went from Ljubljana to Prague. He was suffering from a cold and when the passenger in front of him lent forward to get something, Moby reached over and tore away the paper towel that was there to hygienically protect his fellow traveller's head, and used it as a crude tissue. So the ethos was that Moby's space was to be respected but fuck the personal space of other human beings. In Prague, Moby lectured the local inhabitants on how ecologically unsound their Trabant cars were, not realising that not every country had the United States' level of freedom and industrialised society. I was unimpressed by a spoilt American like Moby, unaware of those people's all-too-real struggles, passing comment about what they did and how they went about discovering their long-overdue freedom.

Driving in and out of these newly independent countries, such as Slovenia and Bosnia, was a strange experience. We spent three hours at a newly established checkpoint, where there were trains packed to the rafters with sheep and cows, with carriages that seemed to go on for days, and an enormous queue of cars, trucks and coaches waiting to get their papers. Some of the countries or mini-states were so small that you would seemingly drive for a couple of miles, stop at a new established border point where your passport would be scrutinized, only to drive on for five miles, at which point you would have your papers checked again as you entered another country.

Once we had absorbed the bombshell that Mute had not picked up the fifth and final option on the record deal, and had effectively dropped us, we regrouped and had a meeting. We discussed the fact that it was imperative that we suppress the fact that we had been dropped, because once it became common knowledge it would be harder to chase and negotiate a new record deal because the press and the business would be writing us off.

In December of 1994, Julian from CEC attended an *NME* Christmas party where he let it slip that we had been dropped. He even gave them an unwitting quote about how Mute had passed on it because the subject matter of the lyrics of the Ed Buller session was 'too dark' to be commercial. Maybe Julian was expressing his own views or CEC's, but it's unlikely that Daniel Miller, who signed dark artists such as ex-heroin addict Nick Cave, gothic singer Diamanda Galás, with her AIDS-themed *Masque of the Red Death* tunes, Boyd Rice with his extremist views or Throbbing Gristle, with their back-projection films of a man having his penis split in two as part of a sex-change operation, would find our petty fare too dark. You would have had to be sitting in a black fucking hole for that to be so. Incidentally, a black hole was exactly where we were sitting.

So, in commercial terms we were holed under the water line – time for the jackals to make their first bite. Mute suggested that we could go on recording records if we didn't get paid an advance, and shared recording costs, but we weren't going to do the band as a vanity-publishing exercise. Our manager, Peter Felstead, spoke to Saul Galpern at Nude. We went out for a drink with Saul and he eventually offered us a £50,000 deal for a one-off album, but we would have to pay for the recording out of the advance. All that we could see with this offer were problems: wasn't there a conflict of interest between Peter's involvement with partly owning Nude and managing us? The advance wasn't a lot, and we didn't want to spoil the memory of that run of glorious singles, videos and albums.

We limped on, vaguely trying to get other record labels interested. We went for a meal with Nathan McGough who was an old friend of the band, and until relatively recently had been managing Happy Mondays. By this point, he was an A&R man at Island Records. His interest in us as a band had been reignited by a performance he witnessed for a Radio 1 live recording at King Tut's Wah Wah Hut in Glasgow, where we came on to play our designated three songs, and some bloke handed me a lit spliff. I walked right across the front row three or four times giving people blowbacks – so we weren't the stiff old farts pretending to be on Ecstasy that Bez and Shaun had made out we were after all. However, Nathan ominously didn't even have any money to buy his own food, let alone ours, and we had to pitch in and pay for it. It was a busted flush; it wasn't going to happen. Eventually Nathan had a row with his boss, punched him and got sacked, so it could have been a mess if anything *had* come of the meeting. Craig made the joke that we all had a 'sinus' problem, that literally 'no fucker would sign us!'

Around this time, we heard from Mute that they were putting out a greatest hits compilation, so we arranged to have a meeting with Daniel Miller in London. We sat in an Indian restaurant and explained that we had a £40,000 accountancy bill and only £40,000 in the bank. We said we would be happy to promote the record with maybe a new single and a tour round the UK and Europe to support the release, but, with no cash flow from publishing and recording royalties, it would be difficult for us to bankroll the gigs. We ventured further and said that, if Mute could lend us a sum of, say £25,000, to help clear the accountancy bill, we could support the release. Daniel stated firmly that we were just too much in debt, that the record deal was too un-recouped. I left the meeting furious. I drove the lads back up the M1 and the M6, biting my lips, trying to suppress tears of frustration, rage and sadness. I said to the rest of the band that if Mute couldn't help us financially, then we should boycott the greatest hits release.

Eventually, by the spring of 1995, Graham insisted that we close our office in New Mount Street, and make Debbie redundant but retain Brenda to do book work, partly because we needed to and partly because we were all intimidated and a bit scared of her. We went on paying Brenda £150 a week for another eighteen months because no one would grab the situation by the neck and deal with it. Eventually muggins rang her up and, in the words of Douglas Adams' whale in the *Hitchhiker's Guide to the Galaxy*, said, 'So long, and thanks for all the fish.' She was nice as pie, and I wondered why I hadn't made the call some £11,700 earlier.

We boycotted the release of the hits compilation, and I only really had limited input in the situation. I rang up Paul Taylor, the production manager of Mute, a really helpful, good bloke, and he told me that, in the absence of our involvement, they intended to name the record *Cow That's What I Call Music* as a pastiche of the *Now That's What I Call Music* brand. I warned him that the band would slate the release to our fans if they dared to call it that. It was funny,

Daniel had persuaded us to avoid signing to a major label in the summer of 1989 with the words 'So you want to give it all away do you?' and we had signed to an indie who were now treating us just as badly, if not worse, than a major might have done in the circumstance.

The record was renamed – uncontroversially – *The Singles*, and the aqua blue cover contained a hideous, distorted Inspirals cow, which the graphic artist had clearly tried to make look 3D. The front cover had a swirling logo that uncomfortably copied the original Oasis logo a little too much for my liking. The running order on the back of the sleeve was different from the actual one on the CD so unknown numbers of DJs all over the world didn't get what they bargained for when they selected track 17 for 'Saturn 5'. This still happens today. Don't blame us – we weren't there.

During this process, we were repeatedly told by folk from Mute that our attitude to the release of *The Singles* would improve once the money started flowing in from sales. It didn't, though. I still hate that release – it's shit. We would have to wait until 2003 for a proper, decent compilation to be released.

We had a meeting in May of 1995 at Graham's house, where he, Clint and Craig all said that it was time to call it a day. Martyn and I wanted the band to continue. I used the analogy that, when a prize fighter gets knocked down for the first time, he might be shocked, but instinct tells him that he has to get straight back up again. Craig said, with finality, 'This fighter's staying down.' I begged the rest of the band to continue, but they wouldn't, and that was that. Two kinds of marriages in my life were now in trouble, my literal one and my musical one.

I don't blame Graham for wanting the pain to end – he had started a bedroom band in 1982, built it through a succession of line-ups (the band has had 11 bass players in all), helped it grow to a massive success and sell millions of records. It must have been heartbreaking to have seen it crash and burn. I respect him for that decision.

A few months later, I was sat in my Mercedes 380SL, which was parked in the garage of my Darley Road house in Old Trafford. I was barely thirty years old, with three children under the age of four, and redundant. I couldn't get a job at Safeway's because people would laugh at the old washed-up pop star. For a few minutes I contemplated sticking a hosepipe in the car's exhaust and killing myself. A combination of emotions, including a sense of the ridiculous, cowardice and fear kicked in and I went back in the house and played with my toddlers.

*VI*
*Keep the Circle*

# 32

## You once had a home,
## a job, a family and pride

My car got broken into, and my wallet stolen. The thief used my credit card in Identity clothing store in Affleck's Palace, so I went in and had a word with them. While I was in there I noticed that there were a few empty units. I went home and suggested to Alison that I should rent a unit and sell Baylis and Knight's women's club wear in it. I was sick of the infighting present at the end of the Inspiral Carpets era. At times over the last months of the band it had almost felt like you had to ask four other people's permission before you could take a shit, so the prospect of running my own clothes shop seemed quite novel and attractive. It wasn't rock and roll, but it could be fun, remunerative and mine. I opened Mad Dog Clothing in the autumn of 1995.

Running the shop was a bit like being a serial bigamist: a woman would come in, I would woo her into buying an item of clothing, then she would leave, and the affair would be over until the next woman came in and the whole process began again. One day a beautiful black woman came in and tried on a sheer see-through dress and stood their virtually naked, with her Amazonian breasts swinging gently, teasing me with a direct smile and asking me, 'Are you going to the Haçienda tonight?' I went dry in the throat as I gasped that, unfortunately, I wasn't.

Around the same time that I opened the shop, I also signed with a temping agency because I needed some regular income to pay the mortgage. The agency sent me to work at a call centre in some impressive old mill buildings near Piccadilly in central Manchester. The business ethos was based on the old sweatshops that had previously been housed in the buildings, in that a lot of the workers were middle-aged women or camp men. They would go home early on a Friday afternoon, another hangover from textile, sweatshop days. I didn't go out of my way to tell fellow workers that I had been the singer with Inspiral Carpets, but I didn't deny it if folk asked. Once they found out I had been in a successful band, some of them accused me of putting on airs and graces but I didn't ask, or want, to be treated differently from anyone else.

As I struggled to adjust to my new situation, I found some comfort and solace by eating my way through a chocolate edition of Trivial Pursuit. Each chocolate had a question printed on its foil wrapper. Whilst wolfing down the last one I spotted the following question: 'What band did Noel Gallagher roadie for?' I laughed out loud at the incongruence and irony; there seemed no way to escape my current place in the universe.

# 33

## I want to be you

I had been doing some exploratory songwriting and recording with my friend Jem Kelly. Jem had been in two Liverpudlian bands in the mid-eighties, The Wild Swans and The Lotus Eaters. I first met Jem in 1988 when he and I were travelling in opposite directions – he was re-skilling, moving from being a professional musician towards completing a degree and teaching, whilst I was playing with my band Too Much Texas and steadily heading towards Inspiral Carpets and a pop music career. Over the next five or so years we discussed producing music together.

When I was recording the final Inspiral Carpets album, *Devil Hopping*, in 1994, I would often supplement an eight-hour day in Parr Street studios in Liverpool by turning up at Jem's flat on Hope Street, and spending another three or four hours distracting him from his dissertation by writing music with him. Jem was weary at this time, having got frustrated by the ending of his two bands, and he didn't really want to be in a band again. Who could blame him? Toiling at rock's cliff edge when you have had success and it's all gone sour can be a thankless task.

In May 1995, just as Inspiral Carpets were ending, Jem and I attended a concert by Portishead at the Blackpool Tower Ballroom. It was a wonderful experience, with back projections playing on the wall behind us. Caught up in the majesty and the magic of the moment, we decided there and then that we would start a full-blown band, rather than merely continue with our electronic project. We called the putative band The Lovers, after the Harold Pinter play (or a seventies sitcom with Richard Beckinsale and Paula Wilcox if you prefer).

We recorded two songs in Phil Kirby's studio on Blossom Street in Manchester city centre, in the building which had been Out of the Blue studios where Inspiral Carpets had recorded the *Life* album. We played the two songs to various record companies with the aim of getting one of them to pay for a demo recording to be made, and ultimately to get The Lovers signed to a recording contract. We persuaded PolyGram Records to pay for a demo session at a studio called The Pink Museum in Liverpool. We auditioned a band, getting a young lad called Chris Livesey to play bass, and a drummer called Iain Kelly.

The morning of 15th June 1996 we were to set off to Liverpool to record the demos, but our gear was locked up at the rehearsal rooms on Jersey Street. We got there for 9:00 that morning so we could pick up the gear, but even though our drummer Iain ran the rehearsal room complex, he hadn't organised the door keys so we drove pointlessly around Manchester city centre trying to locate the bloke who had locked up the place the night before.

I noticed as least five police helicopters in the air over the city, which I thought was odd, and many of the routes around town seemed to have roadblocks. Eventually we decided to wait for the keyholder to turn up at the lock up, and to go and have a fry up in a greasy spoon café in a prefab just off Great Ancoats Street. We went in and ordered the food but I realised I had left my mobile in my car, so I went back outside. Just as I got the phone, I heard a thunderclap. I turned around and saw an emerging cloud of dust rising from above the Arndale Centre. I had just witnessed the explosion of the biggest ever mainland bomb in the UK, planted by the IRA. I went back in and the waitress had just placed four breakfasts on the table in front of the rest of the band. They were in a state of shock, as no one really knew how to act after a bomb exploding. Someone said, 'What should we do now?' Not quite sure what to do, we ate our breakfasts.

Three days later, I caught a bus into Manchester to work in my shop. Once I saw the devastation caused by the bomb, and realised just how many people we knew would lose their jobs, the shock I had experienced on the day of the bombing evaporated and I began to cry torrents of tears. The disruption caused by the bomb led ultimately to my wife's clothing business failing in 1999, and many of the shops in the Royal Exchange and the Corn Exchange going bust. The council insisted that store owners continue to pay thousands of pounds in rent while it was impossible for customers to actually come in and buy anything. At least the Council and the property developers eventually got to institute a lot of the changes and redevelopment that they'd been intending to carry out if Manchester's bid to host the 2000 Olympics hadn't been dashed in 1993. Every cloud...

We recorded the demo, but we didn't get a deal with PolyGram. Over the next two years we played quite a few gigs and were invited to record a song for an album called *Rock the Dock*, which was a benefit album for the Liverpool dockers who were out on strike in 1998 and were being denied union membership by the new owners of the Liverpool Dock. The *Rock the Dock* album was organised by Creation Records, and we performed at a benefit concert for it in London in September 1998. I met Noel backstage. I hadn't seen him for three years. He asked me how I was, and I said something silly like, 'What have you been up to?' Noel reacted by laughing and saying, 'You know what the fuck I've been up to!' I suppose I did, along with everyone else in the country, but here was an ex-associate and roadie who had never accepted me when I was his boss, now expecting me to afford him the personal respect that he had never, ever afforded me.

Chris Livesey and our new drummer Paul Kehoe sort of heckled Noel on stage, which I found a little bit embarrassing, and I bollocked them for it afterwards. This first incarnation of The Lovers folded not long after.

It was around this time when a message came through that Island Records had listened to the demos that Inspiral Carpets had recorded in the relaxed final recording session in Rochdale in 1995, and that they liked the song 'Come Back Tomorrow'. The message suggested that Island might be prepared to broker a recording deal with a six figure advance. This was the pure thick years of Britpop, when Blur and Oasis had taken one another on, when Pulp had made up for twenty years in the indie wilderness and The Verve had reformed to reap the benefits of their million selling *Urban Hymns* album. It made sense for a major record label to try to reboot the Inspirals franchise.

At this time, the relationship between Graham and Clint wasn't great. Graham was DJing at one club in Manchester, and Clint at another. I spoke to Graham and he said that he might be up for trying to chase a deal if it could be brokered easily. On my way to see Clint I met a beggar on the street; I gave him a couple of quid and asked him to wish for my trip to be successful. When I spoke to Clint he said that he wasn't interested in reforming Inspiral Carpets, irrespective of how much money was involved. When I walked back past the beggar, he asked me for money again and couldn't remember our conversation twenty minutes earlier.

So, I was without a band, and the prospect of reforming Inspiral Carpets was temporarily scuppered. During the FA Cup final of 1998, I'd walked into to a guitar shop and, as an impulse purchase, bought a Takamine EN40 Electro acoustic guitar for £700. I'd put it under the bed, where it would remain undisturbed and unplayed for the next year and a half.

## 34

## This is how it feels to be lonely

In June 1997, I was returning from a Lovers concert in Nottingham. We had stayed over at a friend's house, and were just going over the tops on the Snake Pass, the site of the 'This Is How It Feels' video, when I got a call from my brother Andrew to say that my father had tried to commit suicide the previous day – he had taken three weeks' worth of anti-depressants and been sick on one of his lungs. He was in the John Radcliffe hospital and it was touch-and-go as to whether he would survive. Apparently he had recently confessed a bevy of affairs to my mother.

My father was seventy-seven in 1997 – he had prostate cancer, was a serial sufferer from bouts of depression, and a lot of his academic friends had died. He had been having regular periods of delusions and he later wrote up some of the weirder hallucinations as the precursor to a cathartic novel based on his episodes of stark delusional madness. In one instance he imagined that he was planning a space mission that would culminate in a landing on the surface of the sun.

I drove down to Oxford to see him on the suicide ward of the John Radcliffe. He was rambling, talking under his breath, rolling off long stanzas of the Scottish poet Rabbie Burns. He became more aware of my presence and opened his eyes. I don't know if it was his incipient madness or the three weeks' of anti-depressants he had taken, but he was talking in a paranoid way about the secret conspiracy that surrounded him, about the secret agents and journalists that he imagined were perched on every staircase and tall building near, waiting to report on him in a Kafkaesque world.

I knew that he could hear me and understand me underneath the carapace of crap that he was communicating, and I just kept telling him that I loved him. He said that he was a bad father, but I countered by saying that he couldn't have been as he had been an inspiration to me and that in my life I had always had the twin ambitions of becoming a father myself and creating works of art, and that wouldn't have been so if he had been a bad father. Dad said that he had been a bad husband and had cheated on my mother. I told him that up until now I hadn't been perfect on that score, and that although it wasn't ideal, it still didn't make me love him any less.

Facing up to my dad's prostate cancer meant that he could either face physical castration by having a surgical operation, involving the removal of the offending cancerous organ, or go for a chemical castration in the bombardment of his body with oestrogen, the female sex hormone. He went for the latter. Funnily, he became a much nicer old man once the chemical castration had taken place; he started reading books on modern art and watching a variety of gangster movies, the *Godfather I* and *II* being his favourites.

I introduced my father to *The Sopranos*, and he loved it, because it was about the Mafia and the main character Tony had a shrink, just like he did. My dad's psychotherapist was the granddaughter of the Russian novelist Boris Pasternak, author of *Doctor Zhivago*.

Shortly after the suicide bid, my mother applied a bit of tough love to my father. She told him that if he couldn't see that living in their lovely house and being married to her didn't make him one of the luckiest men in all living history, then maybe next time he should succeed. Tough words, but he never did attempt suicide again. Later, she told me that I ought to get back to playing music, as it was where my talent lay, and that I should stop working at the call centre.

In 1999 Alison's clothing business went bust. The chaos caused by the Manchester bomb three years earlier had worked its disastrous consequences and made it impossible for Alison to carry on. We moved the business back to our house in Old Trafford. We had sewing machines and a whole wall of fabric stacked high up against one wall in the spare room downstairs, pressing machines and button holers in the cellar, and I got the attic boarded so that we could put the patterns up there. I decided that it might be a good idea to try to get a small unit for the business to run out of.

I looked down our road and saw that an old one-storey building was for sale. It used to be the Barbara Sharples Dance School that my daughter Elsa had attended. Alison was entirely sceptical at the time about buying it, but I did, and that meant she could work from near home, and that the children wouldn't end up sewing their hands to their mouths with the machines, or dying by an enormous roll of cloth landing on top of them.

I was fairly badly depressed at the time, and probably presented a fairly hateful figure to others. Eventually it became clear that I would have to leave the matrimonial home.

In August 1999 there was a total solar eclipse and somehow the bout of midday spooky darkness affected me very deeply. When the sun came back again I felt as if my life had been reborn, that I was now back in synch with time, the seasons and reality. A similar instance happened when I was sitting in the bath and I could feel the depression weighted on my shoulders. Suddenly it lifted, like angels' wings; it was gone and a muscular lightness had replaced it.

On Bonfire Night 1999 I finally packed my possessions up into four, sad Astra car loads and drove them the three miles from Old Trafford to my friend Jimmy's ground-floor flat in Burnage. My children came to visit the flat, but every time I took them home to their mother I felt the same sickening feeling of separation that I had felt when I had left in the first place.

# 35

## A man is no man if he
## doesn't have the beast inside

Following my mum's advice, I took the Takamine guitar out from under the spare room bed and started to play it. I was beginning to set out on the first tentative steps towards a solo acoustic career. Experience in The Lovers had taught me to play some Inspiral Carpets material as it would be easier to get gigs. Touring solo wasn't making me rich in pocket, but it was cheering up the post-separation blues, and it was sustaining me in the flat I shared with Jimmy in Burnage.

Over that first year I started to market myself across the UK, playing shows in a variety of venues. A club in Leeds hosted me for three Sundays in a row where I got paid £200, and a Sunday lunch to boot. I performed at a club in Aberdeen where the local radio station had played my song 'Inside' hundreds of times, and the whole audience sang along to every word. A stranger gave me a fresh trout as a gift, which I handed to a taxi driver as barter for the fare.

On the night of the Millennium, I performed solo to some 30,000 people supporting Ian Brown at a free concert at the Castlefield Arena. Two friends came on stage and helped me sing a version of the UNKLE/Ian Brown song 'Be There'.

I chose this because it was the song Ian sang when he came out of prison some years earlier, after being arrested for a ridiculous trumped-up air-rage charge, where he called the pilot all the names he had called me at Spike Island. Ian

234

had been rude to me backstage at the seminal Roses gig, partly because I had attended the 'happening' in disguise, with a stubble beard, a hat and dark glasses, not wanting to be hassled out front by the thousands of Roses fans there, and also because although the day was a fantastic event, it wasn't a very good concert – the supports were bizarre and the sound from the stage wasn't very good. Ian knew that I knew this and I knew that he knew that I knew this, and so on. After the gig at Castlefield I stayed out of Ian's way, but he did mouth the words 'thank you' to me from the other side of the stage, which was a nice touch.

I got in touch with an old Inspiral Carpets contact in New York called Neville Wells. He used to promote bands at the Limelight club, so I asked him if I could come and stay at his house and do a couple of acoustic shows in Manhattan and New Jersey. Neville came through for me. In February 2001, I flew to New York and Neville picked me up at JFK and took me back to his wooden house in Kearney, New Jersey.

Neville was living a bit of a chaotic life when I went to visit him, he was drinking a lot, promoting at a Manhattan bar, and taking the odd drug or two. He had cigarette burns on his arms and would wave a lit fag around dangerously near my face. One night I went into town with Neville and at the end of the night he decided that he wanted some coke. I didn't think it was a good idea, but we stumbled around Manhattan at two in the morning while he tried to remember where a contact's house was. Eventually he banged on a stranger's door and a bad-tempered man came to the window and told him to 'Fuck off.'

I played a concert in New Jersey at a small venue where two American über fans turned up called Dennis and Lois. Dennis and Lois have been music fans for forty years and followed Inspiral Carpets around when we had toured the States back in the early 1990s. They used to sell T-shirts for every decent band that went through New York. Happy Mondays wrote a song called 'Dennis and Lois', which appeared on the band's *Pills 'n' Thrills and Bellyaches* album, having met them and probably stayed at their flat when they went to New York in 1988.

I took a trip to Dennis and Lois' apartment in Brooklyn. Their home was full to the beams with vinyl, CDs and what must have been 40,000 toys, including every possible PEZ sweet dispenser you could ever imagine. Lois told me of an occasion when a band member of Doves had been chastised by her because she had found that a sealed, half-full polystyrene cup of Coca-Cola had been thrown away. She had told him, 'But that was Joey Ramone's cup of Coke from 1983, how dare you throw it away?'

Dennis and Lois took me out for a meal, and recounted the terrible story of how they had promoted a North American tour of The Fall, saying that the whole thing had descended into mass debt when the band had a fight on stage at a club called Brownies. Dennis and Lois told me that the following day Mark had hit his girlfriend, Julia, around the head with a telephone handset, and that Steve Hanley, the band's bassist and longest serving member, had flown back to Manchester with just a few hundred pounds. They were furious with Steve. Hearing them talk about Steve Hanley upset me; being in that band for nineteen years must have been at times terrible, and returning to the UK after tour managing the band for years, with a few quid, seemed very sad.

I had seen Steve play with The Fall a few times, going right back to 1983 when I saw them play at the Haçienda. It had been one of the gigs that had made me want to move from Oxford to Manchester in the first place. I had shared drinks with Steve at The Crown Inn at the bottom of Deansgate in the mid-nineties where he had mercilessly teased me about the fact that Inspiral Carpets had appeared on *Top of the Pops* with Mark E. Smith, but The Fall hadn't. I had also appeared at a themed concert at the Night and Day Café where everyone had performed songs by Madonna. Steve played with his new post-Fall band, Ark, and we met and exchanged telephone numbers.

When I got back to Manchester from New York, I rang Steve and said that I wanted to form a new band, and wanted him to be the bass player. We arranged to meet, and that was the beginning of the new version of The Lovers. I recruited Jason Brown to play guitar and, after Paul Kehoe left, Steve suggested his brother Paul for the position of drummer. I irritated Paul at the first rehearsal by saying that I had seen The Fall play in 1983 at the Haçienda with two drummers, Karl Burns and 'some other bloke'. Paul said, 'You cheeky bugger, that was me.' He still hasn't forgiven me for this comment!

The fifth and final member of the band line-up was a girl called Kelly Wood. I had first met her after she rang up in April 2001 and asked me if I would perform solo at a concert she had to arrange in order to complete her music course. I said that I would, and we met some days later. Kelly was an attractive mod girl with dyed blonde hair in a bob. She was also a keyboard player, with a Hammond keyboard at home. I asked her to be the fifth side of our musical pentagon.

We began rehearsing at City College's Abraham Moss Centre in Cheetham Hill, in the music building called the Cook Freeze, so called because it used to be the building where council school dinners were prepared and, yes, cooked and frozen. Over the next nine years, we played over 100 concerts, and actually produced an album, all written and recorded in the Cook Freeze. *Abba are the Enemy* was recorded from 2002 until its release in 2004 on my own New Memorabilia Records.

The Lovers performed their first concert at the Blue Cat

Café in Heaton Moor, near Stockport, on 11th September 2001, another important musical date related to aeroplane disasters. Not only had Noel famously auditioned for Inspiral Carpets on the day of the Lockerbie bombing but Clint tells a story about Meagan's mother which is quite spooky. She worked for American Airlines and part of her job was to counsel relatives of people who had died in accidents. On one job she went to counsel the parents of an English guy who had died in a plane crash and, as part of the process, she got talking to them about her son-in-law Clint being in a band. Of course they'd never heard of Inspiral Carpets, but when she next saw them they had cleared their son's flat out and amongst his possessions they found the *Plane Crash* EP.

Just a few months after the Inspiral Carpets split in May 1995, I was at my daughter's primary school for sports day and I spent thirty frustrating minutes talking to Clint while walking around the playing field kicking the flower heads off dandelions and ignoring the egg-and-spoon races. Clint wanted to pursue a solo career and was worried about our old agreements. Soon the lawyers were involved. Clint's lawyer was sending our lawyer letters and then, realising there was an error in the first letter, would send another correcting it in the second post. I copied each letter and would scrawl on them 'This letter has cost you £250' before posting them direct to Clint.

In 1996 I bumped into Clint and his manager at Hammersmith's Riverside Studios. I asked Clint what he was doing there and his manager said 'I am here to get Clint out of every deal ever made with you.' I explained to Clint that he was free to earn any money he wanted as a solo artist, and that we would never want any of it. In fact, I said, I would personally stand up to defend his money if it was required, but it wasn't necessary to rip up everything we had set up and agreed.

Craig had put together the band Hustler with a collection of musicians formerly in an Oldham-based band called the YaYa's. Hustler played slow, Southern-influenced American-style rock music, along the lines of The Band. Eventually they changed their name to Proud Mary, with Craig sinking a few thousand pounds into the band to help them to rehearse and record some demos. The singer, Greg Griffin, got disillusioned and went off and spent some time on a kibbutz in Israel, and the band reached a hiatus. Meanwhile, Craig, trying to keep some motivation going, sent the demos they had recorded to Andrew Mansi, the old Inspirals tour manager. He loved the songs, and in due course passed the music on to Noel.

Later, to his total surprise and horror, Craig discovered that Noel had actually signed the band, but had replaced him with a session drummer. Craig tried to pursue Proud Mary for the money he had invested in them, but, in typical music business paradox, the band was saying that there was no money in the record deal, while simultaneously their agent was boasting that Noel was spending pure dollar on them to talk up their fees. To make matters worse, when the album Noel had produced with them was released, the challenge and freshness of their early live sound was replaced with bombast and overproduction.

Prior to this, Craig had got involved in an altercation outside South nightclub in Manchester city centre, after some of his mates tried to bring cans of beer into the club. The bouncers kicked off and started to fight with them. Craig tried to get away and was chased down to Kendals department store where one of the security staff caught up with him and hit him over the head with a metal rubbish bin until he broke his jaw and knocked him out. Christ!

Craig had always had a ready wit, and could wind folk up the wrong way, but he never deserved that kind of treatment.

Clint got over the legal tangles and between 1997 and 1999 he had a successful solo career with his band The Clint Boon Experience. They released two albums: *A Compact Guide to Pop Music and Space Travel* and *Life in Transition*. Their song 'White No Sugar' is a classic.

In 1999 I heard an announcement on John Peel's Radio 1 show that The Clint Boon Experience had been involved in a serious crash about forty miles out of Glasgow, near Abington services on the way to a concert at King Tut's. A rear tyre blew out on the splitter bus, and the whole vehicle rolled over seven times leaving two members of the band, Tony Thompson and Kathryn Stubbs, with broken necks. They had to be airlifted to Glasgow Royal Infirmary.

I went round to see Clint in his house in Milnrow some weeks later, and he was still in a state of shock. The seat belt had saved his life; there had been an enormous piece of metal inches away from his face as the van rolled over and over again and ended in an embankment. Once he had crawled out of the van, he found a mobile phone in several pieces and had patiently put it back together in order to call the emergency services.

# 36

## Come back tomorrow

The first piece of press that announced Inspiral Carpets had reformed and were doing their first shows in eight years was eclipsed by a children's TV programme. Richard Jones, who had been managing Clint, used the news of the shows to act as an event to push the fact that Clint had recorded the title music for a children's TV show, *Engie Benjy*. Martin and I were furious.

The process had begun when all of the Inspirals met together in a Manchester hotel. We needed to do a new publishing deal, because the retention on the songs that Chrysalis held for our first three albums had expired. We wanted to replace the frankly rubbish *The Singles* compilation that had been released in 1995 with a proper hits compilation, and we wanted to release an expanded version with rarities. Richard Jones was brought in to negotiate on our behalf.

We worked with Mute on the creation of a new greatests collection. Paul Taylor and Shaun Connon worked with us, two stalwarts from the early nineties days when we were originally signed to the independent label. It was a slow, painstaking process archiving the early Inspiral Carpets material from vinyl to digital transfer. Having thrown my dummy out by refusing to have anything to do with the release of *The Singles*, and being horrified by the quite frankly horrible artwork on the band's second, fourth and singles hits albums, I was insistent that we use Andrew Doran from local design firm Menagerie, who I had used for all my solo singles and albums. So insistent was I that I sent an email to another band member, slagging off the quality of Mute's in-house art department's efforts. Somehow this email got attached to a virus and went around the internet, harvesting its way through all our address books, so everyone (Mute included) got to see my criticism. They *did* let us choose the artwork after this mea culpa.

It was a tricky time for me, I was going through painful and protracted matrimonial proceedings and the situation made me crabby. I was hesitant to agree to the concerts with Inspiral Carpets in 2003, but Richard Jones was skilled at handling people and I eventually capitulated. I reckon all the money I earned as part of the reformation of Inspiral Carpets between 2002 and 2004 went on my divorce.

In the end, despite all the difficulties that come with middle-aged men going on tour, the concerts were magic; how great to go round the UK with your old mates, making so many fans happy and earning good money.

A professional and personal high for 2003 was playing to a capacity audience at Brixton Academy. We got The Hornchurch Haverettes back for a return trip to provide their psychedelic marching band accompaniment to 'She Comes In The Fall'. One of the crew had given massages to band members at a concert in Sheffield some days before, and they had inadvertently pulled my left leg out of joint, leaving me in constant pain and making it truly difficult to move around on stage. I still can't watch the footage of the show without connecting existentially with the pain I was feeling whilst performing, but it was a great concert and a wonderful return for us. I looked out at the sea of faces immediately in front of us in the hall and had the weird realisation that a full five years of a solo career, which had involved me playing out to hundreds of concerts all over provincial venues, pubs and festivals, meant that, bar a few, I actually knew all of them.

This mass recognition of a crowd felt like a dream or a weird kind of reverse *Where's Wally?* where the crowd scenes are made up from hundreds of people I know, either by sight, context, or name. This mass cognisance of a performer's audience feels like one of the secret pieces of glue that informs being an effective front man in a band. This is a secret that you have to learn by doing the work, the concerts, the record signings, the chats. There is my sister, over there is that odd promoter from the Midlands, there's Mike Porter, and so on.

Perhaps my proudest moment of the tour was when we played second on the bill of the main stage at Glastonbury Festival. It was immense playing to such a big audience again, mind blowing. The concert was tinged with personal sadness though, as my girlfriend's grandmother had died the day before. We drove down with Kelly inconsolable in the car. I mentioned Gladys from the stage during the performance. After our afternoon show we hung out backstage with the other artists that were playing that day. Craig's daughter, Georgia, had a couple of toy lightsabors and some classic photos were taken of her jousting with Michael Stipe.

We played a sold-out home-town concert at the Manchester Apollo in December 2003. Towards the end of the show, Shaun Ryder came on stage with us and performed a medley of Happy Mondays numbers, which the band jammed to. Shaun wasn't looking very well at that time and this was a comeback of sorts for him; he had been stage-struck for a few years, since falling out with his dad and brother after a Happy Mondays tour that ended badly in 2000. I said to Graham that we had better bring him on at the end of the concert, because once he had beaten his stage fright and actually got on stage, he wouldn't want to come off again.

As prophesied, once Shaun had boogied along to the musical jam for ten minutes, he turned to Clint conspiratorially and said, 'Hey Clint, how about jamming to "This Is How It Feels"?' My heart sank, and, as previously arranged and agreed, Shaun's microphone was switched off and a couple of minders helped him off stage. This was my song to sing, and I didn't give a fuck even if Jim Morrison or Hendrix had at that very moment blustered through time and onto the stage of the Manchester Apollo to double up on the vocal duties, I was singing this one with only Clint for harmonic company.

After the show, the rest of Inspirals were chatting excitedly about what an honour it was to have performed with Shaun, and how difficult it must have been to have countered his demons and get back on stage. I berated them, saying that the honour was Shaun's, that it was a privilege for any singer to sing with them as a backing band, and that they were idiots if they didn't understand such a simple truth. These comments gained agreement, marked in a spontaneous round of applause and cheers from our crew.

# 37

## You can see inside of me
## that something's going down

My mother Ruth nursed my father through a cruel mixture of dementia and prostate cancer from 2007 to 2010. The way in which she cared for him as he was allowed to die at home is one of the most beautiful acts of love I have ever witnessed; she grew stooped and old carrying his lunches and breakfasts up three flights of steep stairs and then down again slowly on her knees with the tray.

My father wanted to die, and my mother nursed him through the last days. His death arrived in the way that a commercial aeroplane circles the airport, lines up against the runway and cuts the fuel before it lumbers down slowly on to the tarmac. Safe. He died in January 2010, aged eighty-nine.

My father should have got an obituary in the *Times*, but didn't. One literary obituary that was published made the point that he 'stepped on people's toes'. Somewhere deep down in my psyche, I realised that his death had set me free of his bullying, and thereby everyone else's.

The Inspirals continued to tour, on and off, in 2003, 2006 and finally in 2008. Craig, Clint and Graham all had young families and complicated lives to balance. Graham was busy working for the promotion firm SJM Concerts, acting as a representative at rock shows such as the *NME* tours. Clint worked his way towards a residency at the South nightclub, which was run by ex-Haçienda promoter Paul Cons, and also a regular slot presenting on XFM Radio. Craig started running a Manchester music tour agency, taking city folks and tourists around the iconic Manchester music haunts, such as the Haçienda, The Boardwalk and Salford Lads Club. Martyn was working at a succession of colleges and also acted as a music advisor for the New Deal for Musicians. I was teaching at Salford University and playing regular solo acoustic gigs, as well as band gigs with The Lovers.

During the rehearsals for the 2008 'Return of the Cow' tour, Martyn and I had wanted to reboot our Cow label and release some new songs. We had swiftly run through a selection of songs, but the vibe was that the core of the band – Craig, Clint and Graham – either weren't persuaded by the songs, or at that time couldn't, or wouldn't, commit to releasing new music. Following the tour, Graham made himself unavailable for band meetings for the next eighteen months. Again, this was something which Martyn and I found frustrating.

During 2009, both Craig and Graham married their long-term partners. At one of the wedding parties, during the small hours of the morning at the Malmasion Hotel, Martin's partner Joanne had a go at Graham, taking out on him mine and Martyn's frustration at the lack of progress with the band. Joanne accused Graham of being a dog in the manger: unprepared to commit to working in the band, but unwilling to leave and allow the rest of us to work unencumbered. Her timing was wrong, and the situation was painfully inappropriate, but the accusation carried an air of truth. I had learnt from a previous experience at Clint's wedding three years earlier – where I had stupidly got involved in a blazing row with Joanne – at all costs, not to argue, and therefore stayed well and truly out of the altercation.

The situation very nearly led to Martyn losing his place

in the band. In September 2010, Graham, Clint, Craig and I attended a meeting at a hotel in Ashton-under-Lyne to discuss the situation. A replacement for Martyn had already been primed. Not long after, I called Graham and Craig, and said that I didn't like the idea, and that one person in an audience of two thousand at the Manchester Academy missing our bald bass player would be one too many. I couldn't get hold of Clint on the phone, or via email, and a pattern of non-communication was emerging from him.

Grudgingly, the band came back together again and we had a series of meetings at the end of 2010 where we told Martyn to keep his girlfriend out of band business. He raised some issues that we had both found frustrating, namely the endlessly delayed meetings and general lack of momentum. I had a few bones to pick with the band myself, as I felt that we should always rehearse every four months or so, in order to keep the band a little more match-fit. I also suggested that we should be more adventurous in terms of the repertoire we played live, and I admitted that we might be getting too old to do the three-days-on, one-day-off tour schedule. In some strange way we were locked in a desperate life-struggle to compete with our twenty-year-old selves.

Within days of the meeting, Graham, Clint and Craig were pushing for the band to do a series of shows around Christmas, with just six weeks notice. The bloc of the band weren't happy when I explained that a series of concerts in small venues such as South nightclub, Oldham Tokyo Project and Fibbers in York (owned by Aaron Mellor, Clint's business associate and co-owner of South) didn't seem like the obvious move for a band who had been away for nearly three years. We had played at the Tokyo Project back in 2006, and the show was disrupted by audience members as it was the home town of three band members. One lad had accosted Craig whilst drumming half-way through us playing 'Joe', requesting an autograph on a CD, and some nurses who were friends of Graham unplugged Clint's keyboard during the gig. The gig was full of love for the band, but it had been hard work, and wasn't an experience that I particularly wanted to repeat.

I spoke to Craig around this time who explained to me that by me refusing to do these shows, I had thrown him into penury, and he'd have to work in a factory making windows over Christmas to make ends meet. In my anger, I remembered my two years of call centre work when Clint, Graham, and Craig had pulled the band's life support the first time round.

We had a meeting in an Indian restaurant at the beginning of January 2011. Clint was tweeting to 16,000 of his closest friends to the affect that we were meeting to agree to do a series of gigs. I tweeted to my modest 400 or so followers that I hadn't agreed to do any shows at all. Graham handed me a list of venues for a prospective Inspirals tour that we could do through his employer, SJM Concerts. The figures didn't seem to add up – the fees were lower than they had been for comparable shows in the earlier tours. I said I wasn't impressed by the offers, and that maybe festivals were what we ought to be pursuing, rather than club dates.

I said I would try to book some shows through the promoters that I had been working with throughout my solo career. Within a week or so, I received firm offers from a dozen or so festivals that wanted us on their bills. I put the offers together and emailed them to the band. There was an issue in that Graham couldn't do one of the shows – The Tunnels Festival – due to his family holiday. I suggested over a series of telephone calls, emails and texts that perhaps we could get a guitarist in to cover Graham for the Scottish festival appearance. I suppose, to be honest, I made this suggestion because I wanted Graham to experience how it felt to have someone suggest doing shows without him, as was very nearly the case for poor Martyn.

After a few weeks of squabbling, Clint, who generally kept himself out of the heavy-lifting of band-based decisions, sent out a group email saying that it didn't feel right using a fill-in guitarist because we were a 'brotherhood'. I snapped, and I sent an angry email to everyone saying that if they could only commit to being in a band on the sixteen days of the year that they weren't doing something more important that they were getting paid more money for doing, then they could stick it up their arse. Craig sent a rejoinder to the effect that we were all fucking knobheads for arguing. In the heat of anger, I sent a tweet saying that the band had split up, and wishing good luck to everyone in their solo careers.

The following day Graham rang me up, furious, asking whether it was me who had sent the offending tweet. I confessed that it was, so he told me to take it down. I agreed, but admitted that it would have been read by thousands of people by now. Graham pushed me to admit that I had left the band, which I refused to do over the thirty minutes or so of the phone call. I told him that I regarded Clint's 'brotherhood' email to have been hypocrisy of the highest order. I said that I would cancel all the shows within forty-eight hours unless someone got in touch with me. Of course they never did. The next day Clint tweeted that the band hadn't split up, but that it appeared that one member had left.

Over the next few weeks I got an email from Craig, Graham and Martyn saying that they couldn't work with me anymore. Graham insisted on having all the paperwork for the band and the operating company back, even inviting himself round to my house to get it. He also made it clear to me that the rest of them had no desire to speak to me, apologise, or accept an apology from me for sending that stupid tweet.

I realised how sick of me the rest of the band must have grown over the years, that maybe I had become too difficult to deal with. Perhaps I had too many recriminations lying under the surface, like a shopping trolley hiding under the skin of a lake waiting to spike anyone foolish enough to dive in head first. As the summer went on I started to hear rumours that the band had recruited their previous singer, Stephen Holt, back into the band. He was actively discussing it on Twitter with Graham.

I was holed up in a guest house in Southsea on 14th July when Rupert Murdoch was questioned in front of a select committee about the *News of the World* hacking celebrities' mobile phones. In the evening I was watching Gavin Esler on *Newsnight* talking about the day's political proceedings, when he wound up the show with the following extremely odd statement:

> 'The Select Committee not investigating
> phone hacking properly would be a bit like
> the Inspiral Carpets going on tour without a
> full line-up.'

At first I thought I had imagined the comment, but pretty soon people started sending me messages about it. There is a habit of some people tweeting current affairs shows and the presenters reading snippets out on air as a sort of conspiratorial joke. I realised that someone out there knew the band were touring with Stephen, and that they had just informed the world. Maybe Esler was a fan and knew one of the band – either way, what a way to find out!

I was summoned to a meeting with the band on 31st August 2011 at 10am at a hotel in Ashton-under-Lyne, the same one we'd met to discuss sacking Martyn less than a year previously. I parked my car in a large space in the middle of the car park, suspecting a walk of shame was in the offing. Arriving in the bar I met Graham, carrying a tray of teas and coffees. I held the door out for him, to which he said something flippant and insulting under his breath. Once in the room proper my heart sank at the reckoning that the band had been there some time discussing work post-me – the table was littered with finished drinks. I knew for sure then that the game was up.

I was given a cup of tea that my shaking hand couldn't hold, and I placed it on the safety of the table. After four minutes of small talk, Clint chimed in: 'We have only invited you here as a legal necessity. We have held a directors' meeting and as of now you are dismissed as a member of the band and as a director of the company.' Graham handed me a letter in an envelope with my name scrawled in biro on the front. Clint continued, 'We are doing a tour with Stephen singing.' With tears streaming down my face, I said that I already knew that. I stuck the letter in my pocket and said that I wouldn't be an arse about it. I left the room and took my walk of shame back to the car, and drove away.

At 8:30 the next morning I got a text from Craig saying that I could contact him any time I wanted, the one act of kindness I got from any of them. Then at 9:00am they announced to the world that they were reforming with Stephen singing. Some weeks later Clint announced in an interview with John Robb that I hadn't been sacked by the band, that I had left and shook hands on good terms. 'We would never sack Tom,' lied Clint.

# 38

## So you live to fight another day

So, where did it all begin? Was it in the garden of our house in Frilford, Oxfordshire with my four brothers and two sisters, dive-bombing one another in our parent's rural swimming pool on a summer afternoon? Or was it on stage in front of 80,000 people, headlining Reading Festival in August 1990? Maybe it was in 1975 when I tried to burn my house down?

There were two cellars under the mixed Victorian wedding cake frontage of our old country house, and a deeper one under the older Elizabethan part. We used to have an electric time playing in these underground rooms – there was something exciting and slightly naughty about carrying on in the subterranean edifice of the house – an approach that defied my father's patriarchal grip on the household. While he translated Chekhov upstairs or bled his soul to Wagner at top volume to a cocktail of sleeping tablets and single malt, we cobbled a mad array of blankets, chairs, tables and assorted furniture and cardboard boxes which my brother Andrew transfixed us into believing was an exact copy of the Nasa Command Module that sent men to the moon. We would sit inside the 'module' with lights switched off, with only battery torch beams for comfort, attempting to imagine the millions of miles of space between us, the astronauts, and Earth. Our father was taking a journey inwards, a translation of his soul, language, art and culture, while simultaneously the next generation took a journey figuratively outwards in the opposite direction, right under his feet.

My sister Helen and I were given the weekly job of taking the rubbish from the various rooms in the house to the end of the garden, where we'd tip it out and burn it all. Helen and I also started to collate spare cardboard boxes and pieces of rubbish into a mock *Steptoe and Son*-style set in the main cellar. One summer afternoon, I placed a small pile of newspaper and a box on the brick floor and struck a match, just as I had been taught to do, week after week, burning all the family's detritus. Ten minutes later, smoke billowed out in a firm, uniform, whitish film, hanging roughly in willow wisps, head height, all over the house. My mother quizzed me, asking me if I had made a fire in the cellar – of course I denied it, and bravely lied. Luckily, the fire brigade weren't summoned on this occasion and for some unaccountable reason, I was never punished for this idiotic action, just as my brother Peter hadn't been, ten years earlier, when he dropped a lit match in a petrol can that exploded and nearly blew his head off.

My brother Andrew found an old pram we had used as babies. He plunked me in it and started pushing me around the garden at great speed, careering down the gravel drive in front of the house, letting go at the last moment so the pram collapsed on its side, crashing to the floor. He then built ramps and spun me over them in an Evel Knievel style. A final twist was to set fire to the pram, with me in it, and then send it flying over a ramp made out of two planks of wood and an up-turned wheelbarrow. I remember sticking a cartoon character from my DC Thompson comic *Sparky* upside down on the inside of the pram, in the misapprehension that it would be the correct way up, and righted, once the pram was upside down.

Punk arrived for us in rural Oxfordshire like a salvo of Spitfires. The first warning of change was in the release of Dr. Feelgood's debut album *Down by the Jetty*. My brothers Martin and Andrew bought the record from Woolworths the day it came out, stuck it on our cheap battery stereo, and cribbed the chords and notes in hurried excitement. Here was something fresh – no more albums by Yes or Emerson and Lake and Huntley and Palmers, no more having to do a three-year Open University doctorate before you could be in the correct headspace to enjoy the new Pacific Eardrum or King Crimson album.

My sister Vicky and I bought *Never Mind the Bollocks* from Haken & Bell, the music shop in Abingdon, the day it was released and played it to death. Vicky and Helen were über-fans of Graham Parker and the Rumour, and were captured for posterity on the record cover of Parker's infamous single 'Hey Lord, Don't Ask Me Questions', pointing out from the front row of the standing audience. Radio 1 banned the single because some bishop complained about the anti-religious nature of the lyrics.

Punk for me was a rejection of the past and its codes, and it told you that you could do it yourself. My first band, Albert Park and His Playmates, was formed while still at my primary school, Garford and Frilford, out in the sticks on the road between Frilford and Wantage. The school had only twelve pupils when I left. Albert Park's most famous accolade was to get a mention in the classic punk magazine *Sniffin' Glue*, where they included a picture of a load of punks at a urinal and the caption said, 'Some people who aren't fans of Albert Park and His Playmates'. We once played a free concert in Albert Park, to which no one attended – we had stuck a self-made poster up on one of the trees, but when we turned up to play, someone had torn it down.

Punk rock and new wave was central to my formative

years. The Sex Pistols, The Stranglers, The Buzzcocks, The Ramones, Magazine, Joy Division, Siouxsie and the Banshees, The Cure, Stiff Little Fingers, The Ruts, Devo, Ian Dury and The Blockheads created the soundtrack to my childhood.

I loved Ian Dury and The Blockheads and Devo for their attack on the mainstream and able-bodied. To a feeble, low-esteemed dyslexic, who had a negative body image like me, this was manna from heaven. I had read the classic John Wyndham science fiction novel *The Chrysalids* as a teenager, a book set in a post-nuclear apocalypse where the offspring of the irradiated are weeded out by the elders of the tribe if they possess damaged DNA. Culling is done in order to protect the 'pure' human genetic stock. I wanted to be one of the outsiders in the Chrysalids, I wanted to be in the book, and go off to the weird flying city, and in my head, so did Devo and so did Ian Dury, because their art, music and ethos would have led to their extermination in Hitler's Germany or Wyndham's post-apocalyptic world.

That's where it all started for me; feeling an outsider and being misunderstood. Punk is in my bones, it affects the way I see politics, the economy, the media, and childcare. Everything. Punk was a gift, and I have only realised its effects on my life by writing this book, a rock thrown into the still pond of our lives, the ripples and counter ripples still falling backwards over one another for ever... strike a match and see what happens!

# Acknowledgements

I've written this book over a period of four years; in hotel rooms, on trains, at home, on planes, whilst swimming, in the gym and on car journeys to the 140 or so solo concerts I perform each year. Ironically for a singer, it is only in the writing of this book that I have actually found my voice.

I want to thank my wife Kelly for all her love, humour and tireless support, and for editing and translating my words from Hinglish into something resembling English. I want to thank Selwyn and Isabel from Route for their enormous help, humour, intelligence and for publishing the book; my family for being lovely; my children Holly, Elsa, Lillian and Sarah for being the sort of human beings likely to sort the world out from the horrible shitty way we have left it for all of them; Inspiral Carpets, that's Graham Lambert, Martyn Walsh, Craig Gill and Clint Boon, for having great musical souls and being funny as fuck and being my brothers; The Lovers, that's Stephen Hanley, Paul Hanley, Kelly Wood, Jason Brown and Andrew Tarling; my friends Jem Kelly, Peter Marshall, Jason Mickley, Paul Fox, Pedro González; my brother Martin and to my mother for carrying those heavy trays ON HER KNEES that even I couldn't lift up and down the stairs.